WITNESSES

WITNESSES

Life in occupied Kraków

Miriam Peleg-Mariańska
and
Mordecai Peleg

With a preface by Rafael Scharf

London and New York

First published in 1991
by Routledge
11 New Fetter Lane, London EC4P 4EE

Simultaneously published in the USA and Canada
by Routledge
a division of Routledge, Chapman and Hall Inc.
29 West 35th Street, New York, NY 10001

© 1991 Miriam Peleg

Set in 10/12pt Palatino by Witwell Ltd, Southport
Printed and bound in Great Britain by T J Press (Padstow) Ltd,
Padstow, Cornwall

All rights reserved. No part of this book may be reprinted or reproduced or utilized in any form or by any electronic, mechanical, or other means, now known or hereafter invented, including photocopying and recording, or in any information storage or retrieval system, without permission in writing from the publishers.

British Library Cataloguing-in-Publication Data

British Library Cataloguing in Publication Data
Peleg, Miriam
Witnesses: life in occupied Kraków
1. Poland. Jews, history
I. Title   II. Peleg, Mordecai
909.04924

Library of Congress Cataloging-in-Publication Data
Peleg, Miriam.
[Mi-ḥuts le-ḥomot ha geṭo. English]
Witnesses: life in occupied Kraków/Miriam Peleg and Mordecai Peleg: with a preface by Rafael Scharf.
p. cm.
Translation of: Mi-ḥuts le-ḥomot ha-geṭo.
1. Jews—Poland—Kraków—Persecutions.   2. Holocaust, Jewish (1939-1945)—Poland—Kraków—Personal narratives.   3. Peleg, Miriam.   4. Peleg, Mordecai.   5. Kraków (Poland)—Ethnic relations.
I. Peleg, Mordecai.   II. Title.
DS 135.P62K684413   1991
940.53'18'094386—dc20   91-3688

ISBN 0-415-06523-2

To the memory of the murdered members of our family, of Józef Szabad, executed by the Nazis in Ponary, Roza Gawronska, who went to her death with her orphans, and in honour of our comrades in the common struggle

Who walked through Poland's days of carnage,
And was a Jew from the dead arisen,
Made wiser by the death which he survived,
Must feed the flames like an apostle.
                              Stanisław Lec, *Anno 1943*

For a long time, I have wanted to write about certain people whom I knew, about certain events in which I took part or of which I was a witness, but although I took up this work many times – sometimes unfavourable circumstances stood in the way, sometimes I doubted whether I should be able to evoke this person or that image, which had faded with the passage of years – I wondered whether I could rely on my memory. Now, however, I undertake this book – it is impossible any longer to delay.
                              Ilya Ehrenburg, *People, Years, Life*

CONTENTS

Foreword by Antony Polonsky   xi
Preface by Rafael Scharf   xii
Translator's note   xviii

1 THE BEGINNING OF THE ROAD   1
2 ON THE KRAKÓW–TARNÓW–LWÓW LINE   31
3 WE BORE WITNESS   46
4 SOME OF OUR CLIENTS   57
5 FUGITIVES FROM THE JANOWSKI CAMP   72
6 COUNCIL FOR JEWISH AID ('ŻEGOTA') IN KRAKÓW: FIRST STEPS   80
7 I DID NOT KEEP A DIARY... SCRAPS OF MEMORIES   94
8 NEW CONTACTS – NEW METHODS   97
9 PARTING   123
10 JANKA'S WANDERINGS, WANDA AND JADWIGA   129
11 THE REFUGEE FROM AUSCHWITZ   136
12 THE STORY OF A CELLAR   142

WITNESSES

13	CONTACTS WITH WARSAW	148
14	FOR WHOM THE BELLS OF VICTORY TOLLED	162
	Appendix	167
	Index	179

THE AUTHORS

Miriam Peleg-Mariańska was born on a farm belonging to her parents, not far from Kraków, where she spent her early youth. She could not afford to pursue her studies at Kraków University but her undoubted literary talent got her a job as an editor of the children's supplement of a daily newspaper in Kraków, where she published many stories and poems.

She was active in the youth organisation of the Polish Socialist Party and these contacts enabled her to join the Polish underground in Kraków during the war – which is the subject of her book.

Immediately after the war she directed the work concerning the surviving children under the aegis of the Jewish Committee. She was a member of the Jewish Historical Institute then active in Kraków and wrote prefaces to their various publications.

She emigrated to Israel in 1949 and for twenty years worked for the 'Yad Vashem' – the National Remembrance Authority in Israel.

Mordecai Peleg, the co-author of the memoir, in which he plays so large a part, was born in Tarnów, where he finished at trade-school. He later owned a small business in Bielsko.

Self-taught, well versed in Polish and Yiddish literature, his appearance and behaviour belied his origin and enabled him to be very effective in bringing help and succour to his fellow Jews during the war – many people owed him their lives.

In Israel, after the war, he devoted a great deal of his time to collecting and recording evidence of the Holocaust.

He died in 1986 and left behind valuable documentation, so far unpublished, of his adventures in Hungary in the years 1944–5.

FOREWORD

This finely written memoir, produced together by a husband and wife team, is a unique contribution to the literature on the fate of the Jews under Nazi occupation. There are many accounts of the life of Jews under the threat of annihilation – memoirs, diaries and historical works. There are also a few works, most of which have not been translated into English, on the body established by the principal Polish underground organisation to aid Jews in hiding on the 'Aryan' side. This body, the Council for Providing Aid to the Jews, known by its cryptonym 'Żegota', operated in a particularly difficult environment, since the penalty for providing help to Jews was death. What makes *Witnesses* unique is that it is an account of the work of the Council for Aid to the Jews by two of its members who happened to be Jews. They were a young Jewish couple, with impeccably 'Aryan' looks, living on the 'Aryan' side, on false papers and actively involved in the work of the socialist underground in Kraków. The picture which they paint of the problems they faced in aiding those Jews who sought refuge outside the Nazi-created ghettos is complex and convincing. They show both the widespread character of Polish anti-semitism which led to an indifference to the fate of the Jews and also the heroism of those Poles who were continually prepared to risk their lives to save Jews. It is a major contribution to our understanding of the mechanics of the Nazi 'final solution' of the Jewish problem by mass murder and of the controversial problem of Polish–Jewish relations during the implementation of this Holocaust.

Professor Antony Polonsky
London School of Economics

PREFACE

The extermination of the Jews by the Germans during the Second World War has given rise to an explosion of writing in all branches of literature. Small wonder, since the greatest crime in history was committed against the People of the Book: who could count how many potential successors of Heinrich Heine, Franz Kafka, Osip Mandelstamm, Isaac Babel, Sholem-Aleichem, Julian Tuwim, Bruno Schulz, Bashevis Singer, Simon Dubnov or Heinrich Graetz have been turned to ashes, irreversibly diminishing the genetic pool of creativity of mankind? The view is sometimes expressed that this flood of words creates a barrier rather than a bridge; that there is too much of it. Such a view is not tenable – what could 'too much' mean in this context? On the contrary, there is a categorical imperative to continue to record, to relive, to analyse, to understand, to transmit. Every book, every journal, memoir or poem, every case-history, every document, every scrap of testimony is a gift to the future – and it is all that will remain after us. The direct testimony of eye-witnesses is self-evidently of supreme importance. The time is approaching when there will be none of them left to speak to us. This book is one of the last of its kind.

On 6 September 1939 the German Army entered Kraków and, for the 60,000 Jews who lived there, some with roots extending over many generations, the world which they knew collapsed, overnight, never to recover. Even though their ultimate and not far distant fate was not yet apprehended, the pattern of persecution leading inexorably to their physical destruction

PREFACE

emerged from the start. *Bekanntmachungen*, edicts of increasing severity, pasted on the walls, marked the stages. First, the separation from the rest of the population – all Jews had to wear armbands with the Star of David. Then, the destruction of the economy. Shops had to be clearly marked – an invitation, smartly taken up, to robbery and looting. Money, except for a pittance, had to be surrendered; anything of value was confiscated and not to be destitute became illegal. Personal freedom was restricted – every Jew had to register, was forbidden to change his address, was not allowed to use the railways.

These edicts were brutally enforced and were accompanied by continuous harassment, raids, man-hunts, searches, beatings. Jews found themselves outside the law, a free prey to brutes and scoundrels – of whom there was no shortage.

The next stage came when the Jewish population was locked in ghettos, where the conditions were very harsh and degrading. Escape from the ghetto was punishable by death. Slave labour detachments taken from the ghetto and put to work beyond human strength led to a rapidly rising death-rate. Special work camps, like the one on the periphery of Kraków, in Płaszów, were only thinly veiled instruments of slow destruction.

The pace quickened when the way led through a KZ, a concentration camp proper, where calculated cruelty was the norm and where the inmates were often reduced to walking corpses. And so to the final stage, the extermination camp pure and simple, death-factories which had no other purpose than to gas and burn human cargoes as quickly and efficiently as the state of the art – Zyklon B and the crematoria – permitted.

It calls for a painful mental effort to envisage this apocalyptic world, for which there is no analogy in history. There have been wars, foreign occupation, oppression, persecution and murder on a massive scale; such horrors continue to abound, but it is totally without precedent that a whole people, without exception, should be separated from its surroundings and condemned to death, and that this verdict should be carried out with the utmost efficiency, overriding war-aims and – in view of the magnitude of the task – involving tens of thousands of Germans operating the various stages of the gruesome mechanism of extermination. This is the background against which the story of our authors unfolds. Historical events take on flesh and become more real when seen through the prism of individual lives of people who we think are like us.

Miriam was born and brought up on her father's smallholding, not far from Kraków, from which the family eked out a modest livelihood. Lack of means prevented her from continuing her studies at Kraków University, but she kept her links with the socialist youth organisations and at the outbreak of war this gave her entry to the underground resistance movement and contacts which she was able to put to good use. As contemporary photographs testify, she was a woman of arresting presence – a dubious asset in the circumstances, but, providentially, she was totally free of Jewish features and thereby hangs the whole tale.

Mordecai, born in Tarnów, an auto-didact, a man of great sensitivity and intelligence, clear-headed and self-assured, had no hesitation in deciding what he must do when darkness fell.

These two, separately and at first unknown to each other, but clearly of similar cast of mind, which made them later into ideal partners, assumed roles which, as will transpire, were nothing short of heroic. They themselves remained unaware of this dimension: ordinary people, you might say, who had greatness thrust upon them and took it in their stride, not fearlessly, but by overcoming fear and in full knowledge of the consequences – with the comforting feel of the phial of cyanide in their pocket, since no one knows the limits of endurance under torture. It would have been easy for them to slide into relative safety and merge with the surroundings – with their 'good looks' and impeccable speech, their chances of survival were reasonable.

Instead, whilst being vulnerable in the extreme, particularly the man, they courted constant danger. They plied their errands of mercy in places the prudent would shun like the plague: in railway stations, assisting people on their journeys; in crowded shops which were used to deposit and pick up printed matter for distribution and where they could be recognised by former acquaintances or friends (even those with the best intentions could, unwittingly, be dangerous); in offices, seeking rubber-stamping of fake documents.

Having secured for their wards 'good papers' – an identity card, a birth-certificate, a confirmation of employment in the right firm, there was always the problem of finding a hiding place: for some it was a cellar, a loft, a dark room at the end of

PREFACE

the corridor; for others a place in a convent or orphanage. There followed frequent visits – to pay 'rent', or to deliver the money allowance or a message from the family. Few of these hiding places remained permanent – a careless word, a suspicious noise, a disturbance in the neighbourhood made it imperative to move, and quickly. All this took place under the prying eyes of a suspicious and jumpy population, the Gestapo, the police and hordes of informers and blackmailers. Even reading about it, fifty years on, one's heart misses many a beat and one is challenged to think whether in similar circumstances one would have found the inner resources to act as they did.

In the eyes of the ghetto-dwellers the world outside the wall, on the 'Aryan' side, was normal. Although it was far from that in any accepted sense of the word, its dangers were of a different order, it offered a possibility of survival at least to those few who had the necessary equipment, i.e., the looks, the language and the physical and mental stamina to withstand the terrible stress of the situation, of pretending to be someone else, of never lowering one's guard, of living every minute of day and night in mortal dread of discovery.

One could have the appearance of an angel, yet the tell-tale details which could give one away were legion; the eyes could be cornflower-blue but their uncontrollable sadness was hard to disguise – dark glasses in themselves were highly suspect. Men, of course, carried their death-sentence with them, ready for inspection.

As important as the physical mimicry was the mastery of characteristic Polish forms of speech and behaviour, particularly in religious settings – how was a Jew or Jewess to know when to cross themselves, when to kneel down or get up during Mass – a moment's hesitation could mean that the game was up. The learning of prayers and the minutiae of ritual was imperative.

The masking of one's feeling in public was a further ordeal, testing endurance to a breaking point, particularly after the details of the death-camps became known. How to hold back 'tears by which a Jew is known', how to react when the topic of the murder of the Jews was raised in conversation with the Poles, as happened all too often – to feign indifference, to condemn? Miriam speaks at one point of how, risking all, she simply could not hold her tongue. Mordecai mentions how hard it was to keep up the pretence when a Jew whom he was helping and whom he tried to console, would burst out, bitterly, 'It is easy for *you* to talk . . .'

In many cases the strain proved too much. Having taken the enormous risk and trouble of getting themselves established on the 'Aryan side', some of these outcasts returned voluntarily to the ghetto to live and die with their own people. And how can one come to terms with the situation where a mother and her child, having been given shelter and hospitality by Polish friends, cannot endure the thought that her presence so greatly endangers her hosts that, one day, she simply leaves, never to be heard of again? What were then the feelings of these people?

In their understandable resentment of the misfortunes that engulfed them Jews were often not sufficiently sensitive to the Polish situation and the agonising choices facing their neighbours. Only by comparison with the terminal tragedy of the Jews does the fate of the Polish people appear tolerable. By any other standards their sacrifices, their suffering and their losses during the war mark them out as the great victims of their history – and geography.

The extent and nature of the support given by Poles to Jews in their pathetic efforts to survive outside the ghetto-walls has been and remains the prickliest issue in the post-mortem analysis of Polish–Jewish relations. It is the Jewish perception that, on the whole, the Poles have not emerged from the infernal trial with credit. They are accused, at best, of indifference and, at worst, of abetting the Germans in their murderous design – the notable exceptions being those few thousands celebrated in Jerusalem as 'The Just Among The Nations' and, surely, the many, unrecorded, who did not live to tell the tale. It is revealing, in view of the indictment, that the indifference and hostility came as no surprise; it was what the Jews were led to expect through the many years of uneasy cohabitation – the sowing of hatred would not yield a harvest of compassion.

The Poles counter, with justice, that effective aid on a massive scale was simply not possible, in view of the power and the utter ruthlessness of the Nazi forces, to whom the extermination of the Jews became an overriding war-aim. Giving aid in individual cases was perilous in the extreme and called for readiness to risk one's life and that of one's family – the Decree of 10 December 1942 issued by the Governor General set the

PREFACE

death penalty not only for the Jews caught outside the ghetto but also for all who gave them shelter or aid of any kind. This was no mere threat and many paid the ultimate penalty.

Despite that, in 1942, an organisation was set up by the Polish underground in Warsaw and Kraków, under the name 'Żegota', with a network thinly spreading over the whole of the 'General Government' for the specific purpose of helping the Jews on the 'Aryan side'. The aid took the form of finding accommodation, supplying false documents, distributing money, protecting them against blackmail, reclaiming them by bribes or cunning from the hands of the police or the Gestapo. The activity of Miriam and Mordecai Peleg was carried out under the aegis and within the framework of 'Żegota', and as we know from the evidence available to us, many people owed their lives to this organisation.

In the controversy which bedevils Polish-Jewish relations to the present day, objective evidence is hard to come by. Here the testimony of Miriam and Mordecai is of singular value. Their integrity and trustworthiness are beyond question. Their daily engagement with both Poles and Jews gives them a unique viewpoint from which as true a picture can be drawn as is humanly possible. No study of that period and problem can disregard this case-history.

The purpose of this book, as Miriam Mariańska sees it, is to try 'to express in human language things which are not human'. One cannot know how this will strike the reader, remote from that time and those events. Sensitivity differs and man has shown a great capacity to endure the suffering of others. But one thing will surely come through: it is people like Miriam and Mordecai, living in those consummately hideous times, who allow us to hold on to the belief that goodness has a chance in the eternal contest with evil.

Rafael Scharf
Institute of Polish–Jewish Studies, Oxford

TRANSLATOR'S NOTE

It is always difficult for translators to decide what to do with proper names. Under normal circumstances, they are either left alone, anglicised or they are translated, as far as this is possible. Tradition has it that one tends to leave people's names alone, unless well-known historical personages are involved. This scheme, in the main, has been followed here.

This work, however, due to its particular subject matter, presents the translator with an additional difficulty and a basically insoluble problem. This complication can only be understood in the context of the story, which is that of a Jewish couple, illegally living and working outside the ghetto, using so-called 'Aryan' documents, i.e. pretending to be Christian Poles. It is very difficult for an English reader to understand the importance and significance which were attached to names, both first names and surnames in Poland at that time. For example, certain common international names of biblical origin, like David and Rebecca, did and still do, brand someone as being of Jewish origin in Poland. Ironically, many Jewish surnames sounded German, as Yiddish is principally a German dialect, and were exotic to Polish ears. The author's maiden name, Hochberg is an example. Her 'Aryan' name, Maria Mariańska on the other hand, is very Polish.

This case is further complicated by the fact that the authors emigrated to Israel after the war. Most people who settled there changed their names to Hebrew versions of their former names, or their rough equivalents, whether the original sounded Yiddish or Polish. Thus Maria became the Hebrew Miriam, and Mieczysław the co-author became Mordecai.

All the original sections of the memoirs are headed either

TRANSLATOR'S NOTE

Marysia or Mietek, which are diminutive nicknames of Maria and Mieczysław, respectively. In the English version, the authors' present, Hebrew names are substituted, mainly because they sound more familiar and the English speaker seems to be able to get his tongue around them much more easily. It should, however, be kept in mind that, under no circumstances, could such names have ever been used under German occupation; it would have been an instant death sentence, as the many references to such things in the text make abundantly clear. All the same, they do feel uncomfortable to anyone with a 'nose' for such things. But so do all the remaining alternatives.

Theresa Prout

1

THE BEGINNING OF THE ROAD

MIRIAM

My decision to adopt 'an Aryan identity' was not at that time dictated by necessity. The year 1939 did not yet foretell the grim future and the present seemed, outwardly at least, bearable, particularly for me. When war broke out, I was in the country at my parents' farm, Przybyszów, near the small town of Pilzno, twenty kilometres from Tarnów on one side and eleven kilometres from Dębica on the other. The farm, about a hundred hectares of arable land and meadows, did not belong to us, but to the Carmelite Convent who also owned the large estate, Lipiny, in that area. This patch of land situated only half a kilometre from the main Kraków-Lwów road was - however strange it might seem - an oasis of peace in the first few months of the war. And in fact it was only in the summer of 1941 that my family were thrown out and moved with the other Pilzno Jews. But in those first few years I was little more than a guest in my family home and, to be honest, I only went there for a little break during the first stage of my underground work.

Six months exactly had elapsed since the war broke out, when the first Germans appeared on the farm. They were a group of Wehrmacht soldiers from a detachment stationed in Tarnów. They were in search of fodder for their horses. None of us at the farm wore an armband with the Jewish star, even though this had been the order for the Jews in that area since November 1939, so it never occurred to those first Germans that we were Jews. They bought some hay and straw, and were even a little surprised at how well my mother and elder sister spoke German. And that was the end of this first close encounter with the occupiers. But not everything around us looked so idyllic.

In September 1939, a few days after the march past of the first German units, in Pilzno, as everywhere else, groups of SS men appeared. First to be destroyed was a wooden synagogue, the first casualty was the shames, Moishe Beer, who died trying to save his Torahs from the burning building. Panic spread among the Jews of Pilzno. The rumours preceding the German invasion had fallen on deaf ears. The eternal Jewish optimists, particularly older people, still remembered the Germans of the First World War and the Wehrmacht soldiers stopping on their way to the East, did not seem threatening. On the contrary: they entered Jewish homes for various services, they paid for food and they were not particularly interested in Jews; if they were looking for them, it was only for them to act as interpreters or simply to be able to speak German to someone. Even those first 'black ones', as the SS units were called, had not destroyed all the illusions.

Not many of the inhabitants of Pilzno set out East. 'The black ones' came and went. Life was continuing more or less normally but in new conditions. There is not much I can say about it: we were country people, and country life and work in the fields have their own rhythm dictated by the laws of nature.

I should write a few words here about my father. In the first September days of the war, before the Germans started advancing in a steady stream of infantry to the East, blazing fires and clouds of smoke were clearly visible at night from the hill where our quiet house stood. German bombers were attacking railway lines day and night. Soldiers from the remains of the Polish Army could be seen walking along the main road, while a crowd of refugees was dragging along on carts and bicycles, but most on foot, carrying what was left of their belongings. The atmosphere was of horror and despondency. But our four ploughs, each drawn by two horses, continued to ride out to the fields every morning. It was the season of ploughing in readiness for sowing, and while we, the young, thought it a complete nonsense to plough and sow in such uncertain times, my father kept saying with a farmer's unshakable faith, 'What shall we and our people eat if we do not do our sowing in time?', so he completed sowing twice and lived to see two further harvests until he died in Bełżec.

THE BEGINNING OF THE ROAD

Here is just one moment which, oddly, has stayed in my memory. When that first winter in the war brought official orders to deliver so-called 'contingents' of grain, our modest farm got such a high assessment that it seemed impossible ever to meet the figure. The official document originated in the local County Council in the village of Leki Dolne, situated three kilometres from our farm. Winter was white and beautiful that year, the roads were covered with snow. I still had my skis (before I broke them when the order came to hand them over to the Germans) and I put them on for the last time, I think, and went to consult the village administrator about whom to approach about getting this draconian quota lowered. I shall always remember what this old, wise, peasant friend of our family told me. 'Tell your father,' he said, 'let God let you eat in peace what will be left to you.' They were prophetic words; words of a bad, but true prophecy.

I was influenced to use my 'Aryan papers' – the very term was new to us – for the first time when I met Mietek with whom I later worked in the underground movement and who to this day has been my partner in life. One day, in the first months of the war, a young man with a typically Slavic appearance turned up and brought us greetings from my brother who had set out to the East in September, in the uniform of the 16th division of infantry and who, after his unit was dispersed, had found himself in Lwów. The ease with which my brother's friend was able to get about with the help of the only document in his possession – a bicycle licence in the name of Mieczysław Piotrowski – greatly increased my self-confidence. I did not look less 'Aryan' than this young man and my Polish could not give rise to the slightest suspicions.

For my first journey to Kraków, I equipped myself, just in case, with an identity document belonging to my friend, Jadzia Matyj, whom, at a pinch, I could have been said to resemble. This was a very naive idea. It turned out, however, that I had no need of this document: nobody looked at it, either during my journey or during my stay in Kraków.

Here begins my husband's story. As our fates intertwined in the years of occupation, we decided to write these memoirs in turn. Our names then were Marysia and Mietek. The fragments of our memoirs will be marked by our present names: Miriam and Mordecai.

WITNESSES

MORDECAI

In the house where I lived in Tarnów, lived a certain Józef Piotrowski, a Pole. When the order came out that armbands with the Star of David had to be worn (Tarnów was one of the first towns in the so-called General Government where this order was introduced), I took Piotrowski's Health Service card, removed his photo and stuck mine in its place. This was my first forged identity document. Some time later – all this took place at the beginning of the war – my friend Cesia Holzer, who was still working as a clerk in Tarnów's City Council, got me a bicycle licence in the name of Piotrowski. This card not only had my photograph, but also bore the stamp of the Nazi 'crow' (as we called the German eagle), and this was quite something. In 1940, I obtained through Józef Cyrankiewicz a pre-war identity document in the name of Józef Mieczysław Piotrowski. It was a green document from Lithuania, rather than a blue Polish one. This surprised me a little and I asked our courier, Wanda Nelken, who handed me the document, why this was so. Her reply came as a complete surprise to me. 'For the moment, only Jews receive the blue documents as they are considered to be safer.'

'How do you mean? You don't know that I am Jewish?'

It was her turn to be amazed. 'Cyrankiewicz hasn't mentioned anything to me,' she said, 'and those who were preparing the document could not tell it from your photograph. Anyway,' she added, looking at me, 'it is not just your photo. It wouldn't have occurred to me either . . .'

This was proof to me that blue eyes had their uses in those times and it was not without significance, even if it sounds like a meaningless story: it increased one's sense of security, it boosted self-confidence, and I had occasion later to discover just how important these feelings were.

To the Tarnów Jews who knew me well I was an Argentinian citizen: it was known that I had relatives there. I told my barber that I had received identity documents from my family in Argentina and he spread this information as if he had seen them with his own eyes.

Among the Poles, as it turned out, I had no enemies and no-one bothered me. But I recall a very characteristic incident. After the war, when I met some Tarnów Jews who survived the

THE BEGINNING OF THE ROAD

Holocaust, they told me that Staszek, a taxi driver from Tarnów, was boasting that he saved my life during the occupation. I met him one day and asked him on what grounds he was building his fantasies.

'What do you mean?' He was truly surprised: 'Don't you remember how often I met you when not a single Jew was left in Tarnów and I had not denounced you to the Germans?'

So this was the rescue of which he boasted. This small incident only reaffirms my personal theory: if the Poles had chosen not to notice us – us, meaning Jews living on the Aryan side – many more of us would have survived the occupation. So maybe there was a grain of truth in what Staszek was saying: he could, after all, have denounced me . . .

MIRIAM

Kraków in winter, 1939—40. I found all my relatives in their pre-war flats. The clothing factory owned by my cousin, Dawid Birnbaum, had a German supervisor. The children of my cousin, Berta Schornstein, had been expelled from their Polish school. The Jews were not allowed to travel by rail without special permits. The Jews were allowed to travel by trams only in wagon trailers or in special compartments separated by a rope from those for the Poles and the Germans. A short time after that order the tramways of Kraków were separated yet again – this time the Poles were separated from the Germans. But this had not been foreseen by the Poles, particularly the ones who took pleasure in the Jews travelling separately. I stood amongst them, watched and listened to what they were saying, and sometimes I felt ashamed for not standing on the other side of the rope.

What made up for this feeling was the fact that I was not restricted in my movements by the order for the Jews not to leave home after nine o'clock at night without special permission. And a few months later, in May 1940, I was able to walk in all the 'forbidden' streets and places: the Main Square, the famous Planty Park and the Clothiers' Hall, and I did not need to leave the pavement and step into the road at the sight of a German, like other Jews.

During this first wartime visit to Kraków, I looked up Józef Cyrankiewicz. He had been ill for a time but, knowing him, I knew he would not stay inactive for long. It was useless to ask him about it, I tried to approach him cautiously, but he brushed off my questions. I only learned that he had been taken prisoner by the Germans, escaped from the train taking prisoners to Germany, and was offering advice to his Jewish friends and acquaintances, telling them to escape to the East. He advised me similarly, but I had no intention of fleeing to the East. I don't know why, but he must have been the only one in my circle at that time who had no illusions about the fate of the Jews under the German occupation. That memorable first September of the war, great masses of the Polish and Jewish populations were fleeing the German Army and as I watched them as I stood in the garden of my family home, I would get the urge to join them, so intense and overpowering was the scene. But my father decided that he would not budge. In 1914 he had left his home and farm and on his return found not a single nail on the wall – these were his words – so this time he was determined not to repeat his mistake.

I stayed therefore with my parents while my sister with her husband and two small daughters went 'East' in a cart drawn by a pair of our best horses, loaded with their most valuable belongings and with food. They came back – alas! – and fell into the hands of the Germans.

When I told Cyrankiewicz that I was not going to take his advice, but that I had no intention of staying idle either, he decided that first of all I must get registered in Kraków under an Aryan name. I was to go to Kraków a little later to arrange for the necessary formalities. Thus in the summer of 1940 we both – the false Mieczysław Piotrowski and I – received Polish pre-war identity papers. The name I chose for myself was a most unfortunate idea. I simply translated my family name, Hochberg, into Górska, and I was called Maria Górska, born in Równe Wołyńskie, a Roman Catholic, and a clerk by occupation. My place of birth was also a naive idea, based on the illusion that the Soviets would stay in those territories until the end of the war and it would be difficult – in case of an investigation – to check the details. It was the same with Mietek who was supposedly born in Rokitno in Wołyń. I didn't have the faintest idea what Rowne looked like: I knew very little about that town. Today, after listening to many accounts of Jews who survived on 'Aryan' papers, I know how important such

THE BEGINNING OF THE ROAD

matters were in case of an investigation. But in those days I didn't think about it and throughout the war I never needed to.

From the advertisements plastered on walls of houses, I found myself a place to live, a small room in Mały Rynek (Little Market), which I rented from a certain witch called Mrs D. I do not even feel like apologising for the name I have given her. The room was as scruffy as she was herself, but it had its own entrance from the small corridor and there were no neighbours. In spite of that, the room was not very suitable for underground work because its window looked onto the stairs leading to a wooden porch used by the tenants of the other flats. The moment I started typing out the news coming from London radio in that room, I realised that someone walking by my window could take an interest in the noise, but I must have had 'that little bit of luck'.

To make my stay in Kraków seem a bit more plausible, I enrolled in a German language course to make it appear that I was looking for office work for which knowledge of German was necessary. I always had my books and essays for my 'studies' by me.

I was at the time on the editorial staff of an underground paper called *Wolność* (Liberty) which appeared – if I remember correctly – three times a week. My task was to get every day at seven a.m. the London radio communiqué from 'Piotrus'. By a strange coincidence 'Piotrus' had the same name as my Mietek, only he was a real Piotrowski with a double-barrelled name, which made him Kazimierz Ginwill-Piotrowski. As he had an excellent knowledge of English, he listened at night to the English radio communiqués, translated them into Polish, and gave them to me first thing in the morning. He was as exposed to the dangers of being found out as I was. The entrance to the room where he lived and worked was just opposite the staircase. When I knocked on his door in a special way, I could hear clearly how he – just in case – put away his radio under the bed, then put away the pieces of paper with the London radio communiqués and only then would open the door. This camouflage was, of course, naive in the extreme, and would not have stood the test of – Heaven forbid! – a real German search of his room. However, he was lucky and survived the occupation.

I used to type the radio communiqués on matrices and at a

given time I would take them to a certain shop at Karmelicka Street where our undercover 'letter box' was. The shop and the system of transmitting underground materials have their own story. The owner of the shop was a Mrs Fischer, an 'official' Volksdeutsch,[1] but in her heart and conscience a Polish patriot, devoted to the underground work. Her daughter Danuta worked in the shop and the entire undercover business was managed by a Madame Zofia. I do not recall her full name, but I well remember this spinster, a blonde with rosy cheeks and a slightly nervous manner, which was not surprising – there were enough reasons for her to be nervous.

I knew that an 'Antoni' used to come for the communiqués, typed and ready for copying, but I did not meet him for a long time, because such was the system of our work: we tried to ensure that as few people as possible knew each other. I also had my own system of handing over the matrices when there were shoppers in the store, and one could not be sure that one of them was not an undercover agent. I would assume the role of a regular customer and ask Madame Zofia whether she had put away for me, as promised, some onions or potatoes. Madame Zofia would say, 'Yes, I have put some away for you, they are in a box in the warehouse'. So I would go to the warehouse, leave the matrices in the appointed place and leave carrying – just in case – a bunch of onions or some other safe product. As I have said, I did not know whether the mysterious 'Antoni' was already in the shop at the time or was to come later to collect the matrices.

One day the arrival of the communiqués was delayed because of some important last minute news. I had to collect the scripts from 'Piotrus' in the evening and take them to be copied first thing in the morning, the moment the shop opened. I was there at seven a.m. and found the shop still closed. I walked round for a bit and after a time I caught sight of a young man who, like me, was walking up and down the pavement on the other side of the street. My first very natural feelings were anxiety and suspicion: could he be watching me? But when I looked closer at him, I recognised Janek Rosieński, the son of Mrs Rozenberg-Rosieńska who taught at my primary school in Pilzno. After a moment's hesitation, Janek approached me and greeted me

---

[1] Ethnic German living on Polish territory before the war. [Translator's note]

THE BEGINNING OF THE ROAD

cordially – we had known each other since childhood.
'What are you doing here at this time?' he asked.
'I am waiting for the shop to open.'
Our conspiratorial dialogue continued:
'Which shop?'
'This one here.'
'Do you come shopping here so early in the morning?'
'Yes, today I came early.'
'And on other days you come later . . .
But why are you asking me all these questions?'
'Because I am waiting for this shop to open too and I don't know why it is still closed.'
I was the first to summon some courage: 'Are you not Antoni by any chance?'
Janek's face fell, but he must have realised there was nothing he could do as I knew his pseudonym. 'Are you Ewa?'
I did not even know this was my conspiratorial name, it must have been meant for those who did not know me. But I discovered in this way that he was the person collecting the matrices and taking them to be duplicated. We seized this chance to exchange our addresses – thus breaking all the conspiratorial and undoubtedly sensible rules, and from time to time we visited each other, naturally without our 'boss's' knowledge. Even Cyrankiewicz, who adhered strictly to the security rules, himself put great trust in his lucky stars, which eventually failed him. I did not realise what an important role he played in our underground organisation, until one day I asked idly, 'If we were ever apprehended together, surely we should have some story ready about how we first met?'
'Yes, I agree', he said in his usual, slightly sarcastic way. 'We shall tell them that we met over a cup of coffee at the "Krysztal".' 'Krysztal' was a café where we used to go to read the papers before the war.
Cyrankiewicz knew very well that life or death often depend on luck or chance, while the strictest security measures can often fail. His theory proved right in the case of Mietek and me, but, alas, not in his own.
To return to my landlady in the Little Market, whom I have described in such unflattering terms: a few words of explanation are needed here. She was a typical representative of a

9

section of the Polish lower middle class, imbued with anti-semitism to their very bones. All attempts at analysis fail when one is confronted with this kind of person. Mrs D. went regularly twice a day to church and was a living illustration of the Polish proverb 'paying lip service to God – nursing the devil under the skin'. She used to declare that she would immediately denounce to the police any Jew who came her way. Maybe she would have denounced them to the Polish police because she was a Polish patriot. Among many examples of Jewish iniquity which she used to quote me at every opportunity, she had one which was particularly interesting. She told me that when she had been ill and spent a few days in bed, alone and with no one to visit her – even her only son hardly ever came – she was seen from a window in the main building by a Jewess living there, who came to ask her if she needed any help. During her visit she said – I quote Mrs D. – it would be unthinkable among Jews for someone ill and alone to be left without any help: the neighbours would immediately come to look after such a person.

'But this was rather nice of her', I said.

To which Mrs D., this self-styled philosopher, replied 'This is what they are like, these Jews. They always hang together, always in a bunch, and always against the Catholics.'

It was impossible and in our situation also dangerous to get involved in such discussions. But sometimes it so happened that silence was even more dangerous. For instance, one day my landlady, while cleaning her room, took down in my presence the painting of Jesus Christ on the cross on the wall in order to dust it, and started talking to the painting to the effect that only now the Jews were reaping the just rewards for their crime and that this should bring consolation to Him who suffered so much at their hands. I could not bear to listen to this idiotic monologue and I said, rather forcefully,

'Do you know that if Jesus could get one leg off the cross he would kick you for what you are saying now?'

'Why?' Mrs D. was amazed.

'Because', I said, 'you want to bring consolation to Him who proclaimed "love thy neighbour" by the fact that innocent people, old men and women and children, are being murdered? '

'I can see that you are on the side of the Jews.'

THE BEGINNING OF THE ROAD

'No,' I said, 'I am on the side of Jesus Christ.'

My landlady was too primitive to understand what I said. Her reaction was a few days' sulking, but she had no suspicion of my belonging to this 'vile' people. After that we had a few similar conversations and her reaction was always the same. I was often called 'Jewish aunt' by her or even 'a communist', but I must have been blessed with looks which were impeccably Aryan, and an unshakable self-confidence. This worked to such an extent that later my future Jewish 'charges' saw in me solely a noble Pole. I had many interesting experiences of this kind, but I shall describe them later. The so-called 'Jewish department' in the underground Polish Socialist Party organisation confined itself to spontaneous actions. It was not organised aid and only concerned a few individual cases. It involved mainly providing Aryan documents and – in the few cases known to me – of legalising Jews who could be passed off as Poles in their domiciles and places of work. Three leading underground activists with whom we worked at the time were engaged in helping the Jews. They were Józef Cyrankiewicz and Zygmunt Kłopotowski until their arrests, and Adam Rysiewicz, who was murdered in 1944.

The help given to Jews at that time stemmed from those activists' personal connections. They were concerned with their Jewish party comrades, personal friends, and through them, also about their families and friends. The underground Polish Socialist Party in Kraków had no *placówka legalizacyjna* at the time (an office where documents were forged). As far as I know – and my information came mainly from Kłopotowski who was less secretive than Cyrankiewicz – the forged Aryan documents were prepared by underground military organisations, whose attitude towards helping the Jews was not, as we know, very positive. Adam Rysiewicz acted as courier in those matters and he often had difficulties in obtaining an Aryan document if the person on the photograph had too clearly 'Greek' features, 'Greek' being the code word for 'Jewish'. The most suitable, least suspect, faces had to be chosen and this was not always easy. Rysiewicz and Kłopotowski used the camouflage usual in those days, saying that the documents were meant for Poles, members of underground organisations. Many of them in fact did use two or sometimes even three names. The Jews were 'the infiltrators' in this group and this was why 'good', Aryan looks were so important.

MORDECAI

In 1939, in the second month of the war, I crossed for the first time the then Soviet-German border. I was with a group of friends and relatives, all from Tarnów. We were not far from the village of Bircza near Przemyśl. We were stopped by the Germans, ordinary border guards who took us to a house where there were Wehrmacht officers. They searched us, took all our money, our watches and some clothes. At night they let us go by boat across the river San to the Russian side. From Bircza we got to Przemyśl and from there to Lwów.

In Lwów, total chaos reigned, there was no food, everything was terribly expensive and I was nearly penniless. There was no question of earning money in any way. What should I do? I decided to go back. I got the address of a Jew living near the railway station in Załuż, a village near Lesko. His name was Sprecher and he was a farmer. Sprecher had a wife, two grown-up daughters and a son of military age.

Here, in this very house, his father and grandfather had lived. Hundreds of Jews fleeing to the East had found shelter with this noble family. It was here that I met Makarski, a Pole living in Biała Góra near the Soviet border. Together with Makarski I crossed the border one night and arrived in the home of the Gregorczyk family. These two places were very important to me.

I went back to Tarnów where armbands with the Star of David and special Jewish identity documents were being introduced. At Wałowa Street in Tarnów was the firm owned by the Kraus (Hirsch) brothers. Two of them fled the Germans to Lwów and the third one, David, stayed in Tarnów. This David, a good looking boy with steel coloured eyes, was taken away by two Gestapo men and shot dead for no particular reason. They must have believed that a Jew could not have such an Aryan appearance. I was greatly shaken by this murder. I decided to go back to Lwów. Again, I found myself in Sanok, at the Gregorczyks'. My friend Langsam (who survived the occupation) knew this town: he had relatives there. He introduced me to the president of the Jewish community,

THE BEGINNING OF THE ROAD

Guzik, who was a very decent and helpful man. In his large home Jews, away from their homes and families, gathered or stayed temporarily. War had found them on holiday, sometimes in hospitals or simply travelling and unable to get home. There were many women and children among them, with no money, nothing to live on. At this time, everybody wanted to get to 'the other side', to the Soviets.

In the evening I left that house, distressed by the tragedy of these people and by my conversation with the president. He appealed to me to do something for them. I went outside and from where I stood among the trees 'the other side' was visible very clearly. Birds were flying there and back freely, and I was weak and powerless. I do not know how long I stood there. Night came, there was quiet on this and on 'the other side', not a soul around. I knew that I had to make a decision, to do something for myself and those other people.

I asked my God – Nature – for help, strength, will, for freedom. I sensed, I foresaw that my people were heading for extermination. In 1938 I wrote to my relatives in Argentina that war was imminent and that after the war the only Jews that would be left would be those in photographs. (Later, in 1965, in Buenos Aires my sister showed me this letter.)

That night, on the bank of the San river, I pledged that I would help anybody in need, disregarding all dangers. I kept repeating this dozens of times on 'the Aryan side', when it seemed that the ground was on fire under my feet.

I crossed the border ten times back and forth – not counting the first time over the Bircza river. Each time I promised that it would be the last, that I should not tempt fate anymore and endanger my life, but after a brief rest I would get anxious and start again. I stayed on the German side, I saw my place there. (After the war, in 1945, in my home town of Tarnów, I was approached by a pre-war acquaintance, Maier Israel, who handed me my photograph. I was amazed. I had no idea where he got it from. In the first days of the war I visited friends and acquaintances and two local photographers – Mroczkowski and Bernstein – asking them to return all my photographs to me. I also collected all the films of my photographs and destroyed them.

'Where did you get it? ' I asked Maier.

He reminded me that in November 1939 in Lwów, he had

met me in the street, extremely upset because he had been robbed on the border near Załuż. Some people had taken him to their cottage – he knew where it was – and taken away his suitcase, which was all he had. Sprecher had advised him to ask me to go there with him. I had given him my photo, told him to show it to those people and to tell them that I said they should return the suitcase to him, that I should be there in a few days and would arrange everything.

He now returned my photograph and told me with emotion how out there, far away in Russia, in Siberia, my photo had lain in his suitcase and each time he had opened it and looked at his valuable belongings – his underwear, shoes, etc. – he had blessed me and wished that we would meet like this one day.

MIRIAM

Cyrankiewicz appointed Bronisława Langrod, the wife of Poland's envoy at the League of Nations before the war, to help me edit an underground paper. At the outbreak of war her husband was in Geneva and then found himself in England, with the rest of the Polish government in exile. Bronia and her young son got stuck in Kraków. She was a delightful person, very intelligent and lively, and – for those times – extremely careless. I had a lot of trouble with the stylistic corrections she introduced in her editorial capacity to material ready for print on the matrices. It is enough to have some knowledge of the system of writing on a matrix to know how difficult it is to correct errors on a mould ready for print, but this made no difference to our friendship.

Things got worse with her exaggerated sense of safety. She lived in a very large flat at Karmelicka Street, one of the main streets in Kraków. Because of these comfortable living conditions, the accommodation bureau allocated a room in her flat to a German officer. In order to get to his room, he had to cross the living room. Imagine my terror when I came to visit her one day and saw on the table in the living room a copy of the latest edition of *Wolność* fresh from the press. I could not find the words to express my horror at such thoughtlessness. And dear Bronia, at her most innocent, said, 'Why are you in such a state? After all, he cannot read Polish'.

I had occasion to find out over the years that caution was no

THE BEGINNING OF THE ROAD

guarantee of success, while on the other hand boldness bordering on carelessness sometimes gets away with murder.

Kraków, 1940: my life follows three different paths. The first one is my work in the Polish Socialist Party's underground organisation. The second one is keeping in touch with my family in the village a hundred kilometres from Kraków. The third one is my day-to-day contact with my relatives who still live in Kraków openly, wear the armbands with the Star of David and work for the Germans or in firms run by German supervisors or *Volksdeutsches*.

At my parents', in the country, it is still possible to have a good rest, to eat well and bring back some food to Kraków. The two or three days I spend there seem idyllic. The Germans cannot be seen there, and the only signs of their presence are circulars demanding the delivery of quotas of wheat, potatoes and milk. I never go to the small town of Pilzno anymore as the *Judenrat* (Jewish Council of Elders) has its offices there by now. I avoid old acquaintances as I cannot explain to them why I travel by train without permission, without a pass, without an armband. Finances are becoming a problem: life is not an adventure film where the main characters appear to be exempt from eating, wearing shoes or paying rent. Cyrankiewicz arranged for all the women couriers to get shoes, through his connections with a shoe factory whose managing director had not yet been arrested. But the organisation had no money to pay any kind of 'wages' to its members. Much later, after Cyrankiewicz's arrest, his successor, Zygmunt Kłopotowski, improved the financial situation. This was achieved through trade on a large scale in bread and cigarettes – the latter came from German rations and bread was obtained on forged food coupons which had been printed by the underground printers immediately after the official ones were issued: they were identical in shape and colour to the original ones. The difficulty lay in their registration in various food shops where the name and address of the owner had to be given. Kłopotowski knew a few friendly shop owners where the forged food coupons could be used with no risk. But this was not enough, we had in various ways to be actors, to register the coupons under assumed names and on no account give the real address. This was not particularly safe, but compared to the complication of life on Aryan papers and of the underground work, this was a lesser kind of danger.

The information bulletins which I used to type on stencils and get duplicated, would come back to me as underground newspapers. I delivered them to given addresses but did not know where they went from there. Sometimes I would deliver information or documents without knowing their contents. After the war, Kłopotowski said to me, on his return from a German labour camp, 'You did not know that for a time you were Bor Komorowski's courier'. No, I did not know, as evidently it was best for me not to know. One thing was certain: what I was doing was directed against the Germans.

My relatives and Jewish friends who knew about my work or suspected something wanted to hear a truth different from the one proclaimed by the German radio and the official newspaper *Goniec Krakówski*. What comfort could I bring to these people to whom each day brought new German orders and new restrictions? The Jews were not allowed to walk certain streets, were not allowed to travel by rail without special rail permits. Various regulations were issued about new registrations and an order of 'voluntary resettlement' of those who were not granted a special permit allowing them to stay in Kraków.

Writing down the daily announcements from London radio became a difficult task in the spring of 1940 and not only for reasons of security. The English radio broadcasts brought us no cheer: on the contrary, they depressed us and dispersed all hope of an early end to the war. Hopeful rumours, which were shared by the Jews like bread by the starving, rumours about some common front of all free and mighty powers against Hitler, disappeared like snow in spring. We had to admit that the Germans' official communiqués proclaimed in Polish on the corners of the streets in Kraków were true. Every month of that year was marked by a new advance by the German Army.

In April Denmark surrendered without offering any resistance. The hope that Norway would defend itself successfully against the Germans was dashed after three months. In May came the occupation of Belgium and Holland and, worst of all, in June 1940 the news about the bypassing of the Maginot line and the fall of Paris.

What news could I therefore give to the Jews waiting to hear what Churchill had to say? I typed his great solemn promise

THE BEGINNING OF THE ROAD

that 'God's mills are slow but just' and that in 1942 England would have a sufficient number of planes, with my heart frozen with horror. In June of that year, my relatives left Kraków as part of 'voluntary resettlement'. Some of them went to Wieliczka. The Schornstein family to whom I was closest all this time, went to the village of Michałowice near Kraków. I used to go there once or twice a week, to see my cousin Berta and her two little girls, Litka and Tusia. These children still enjoyed a sort of normal life, they lived in a cottage overlooking a meadow covered with flowers and there was no shortage of food because their parents were steadily selling off items of clothing and valuables which they managed to bring with them from Kraków. How long was this idyll to last? Not long, because Hitler's mills were grinding much faster than those about which Churchill spoke so grandly.

Each of us, underground workers, applied his own security measures when storing or transferring dangerous materials. I used to carry with me a shopping basket as if I was going shopping. Matrices, notes to be typed or papers already published, were at the bottom, and on top I put a few bundles of firewood. It was, of course, a system which would have proved useless in case of a search. Some time later I bought a few paper sacks of the kind used for transporting building materials. They were made of several layers of thick paper glued together, which would hide quite a lot of illegal material. I used to make a roll of such a sack and I would take it with me as if I was going off to do a lot of shopping. But these sacks were most appropriate for concealing matrices and other documents in my flat. I used to put two or three such sacks on the floor in place of carpets, which could not arouse any suspicion (or so I thought) in such humble surroundings. I used to wipe mud off my shoes on those sacks to make them seem useful. But the joke was that nobody ever came to search my flat though I was fully aware that all those naive subterfuges would prove useless if they came.

Today, in retrospect, it seems incredible that we could lead an almost normal life, eat, sleep, wake, get dressed, take trouble with how we looked – which, incidentally, was very important – all the while under the threat of a death sentence and, what was worse, that death, if something should go wrong, would not be the worst alternative. Everybody knew about the way Gestapo interrogations were carried out. Therefore – like all the others engaged in the underground work – I received one day a portion of cyanide in a test-tube made of very thin glass, which could be easily crunched, just in case. I used to carry it with me and occasionally I looked at the small, grey lump of this stuff which could instantly save me and perhaps others from unnecessary suffering. As years went by, the contents of the test-tube became darker and turned into a powder. I don't know whether it would have still performed its task. Fortunately I never had to use it.

In the spring of 1941, I met Zygmunt Kłopotowski through Cyrankiewicz. This was shortly before the big blunder in Kraków when Cyrankiewicz found himself among the many activists of the military and civilian underground arrested. I often thought about it, that there was something strange going on, a kind of instinct on which many people in those days came to rely in their everyday lives. Sometimes the choice of street or of the time of leaving the house, or a sudden decision to turn left or right into a side street rather than go the usual way, could save one from a round-up which was just taking place there.

Kłopotowski told me some time after Cyrankiewicz's arrest that Cyrankiewicz had asked him to look after me. It could be that he then told him I was Jewish and for this reason should not take part in the most dangerous assignments. As a matter of fact, after Cyrankiewicz's arrest, Zygmunt did take me out of active work for a while and even told me to move to a new place.

I was extremely depressed for a time. Cyrankiewicz was a man who always seemed to me to be so confident, so cavalier about danger, and inspiring such confidence in others by his attitude, and he had fallen into the hands of the Gestapo. For me it was a cataclysm, my peace of mind was shattered. Kłopotowski left me only a fraction of my former underground work, but he started to employ Mietek and me on various 'missions' concerning the fate of the Jews who were in hiding or intended to go into hiding.

I had not quite left my place at the witch's in Little Market. I was registered there, I paid my monthly rent regularly and I

THE BEGINNING OF THE ROAD

thought up various reasons as to why I wasn't there most of the time. I did occasionally spend a night there.

I didn't know that Kłopotowski had been told I was Jewish until one day during a walk together – we often went for a walk just to discuss various things – we stopped in front of a poster announcing in Polish and in German that 'Jews leaving without permission the district of town to which they have been allocated, are liable to be punished by death'.

'And you, have you got such a permit?' he asked, half jokingly.

I was not capable of reacting quickly and in the same vein. I must have looked uneasy, because he quickly said that my looks were my best identity documents. He also admitted that had he not been told by Cyrankiewicz, it would have never occurred to him that I was not a Pole. And a Pole – he added – from the aristocracy. This was no mere compliment, it was a bonus which increased my self-confidence and feeling of security. But even with such a bonus, I could not forget even for one moment that I had lived in this very Kraków for six years before the war, that many Jews and Poles knew me here, and that documents and even the best 'gentile' looks would be to no avail if someone reported me to the Gestapo or simply denounced me to the nearest Polish or German policeman. In fact, no-one gave me away during the more than five years of occupation, when I walked in the streets of Kraków or travelled by train, usually carrying some sort of incriminating item. It must therefore be said frankly and in all honesty that it was not just a question of luck, although this undoubtedly was on our side.

Kraków was not as contaminated as Warsaw by the plague of informers and *'szmalcownicy'*, the blackmailers and extortionists who preyed on people whom they recognized as Jews. I used to meet in the street all sorts of acquaintances. I am not talking here about people whom I considered absolutely trustworthy, but people like shop girls, waiters and, above all, daily helps of my relatives who had been expelled from Kraków. It was they whom I feared the most, not because they were hostile, but on the contrary because of the warmth of their loud greeting in the street whenever they met me, 'I am so happy that you are alive, Miss Marysia! And what happened to Berta, master David, Salusia, Moniek?', and so on. Such non-gentile names spoken so loudly in the street could easily attract someone's unwelcome attention. Polish acquaintances who sometimes passed me by without a word of greeting, would justify themselves after the war: 'We did not want to frighten you, we knew you were distrustful of us.' It is true, we were distrustful. We had, on the one hand, friends on whom we could rely and co-workers in the underground and, on the other, a faceless crowd of passers-by whose ideas about Jews daring to walk the streets openly could be unpredictable. Often, such chance meetings could end badly.

Once, a young girl approached me at a tram stop and asked in a low voice about the fate of my brother, her fellow student from the Commercial Academy. I didn't know her, I had never seen her before and I didn't want to blow my cover.

'I don't know who you mean', I said. I could see her genuine surprise.

'You are not Morycek Hochberg's sister? ' she asked.

'I don't know who you mean,' I answered, sharply this time, and the girl looked very embarrassed.

'I am sorry,' she said, and I sensed that she did not believe me, but I think she understood why I was lying. Kraków was already '*Judenrein*', free of Jews, by then.

One day, I came across Fraülein Lonia, a German governess of Jewish children in a wealthy household before the war. German governesses from Silesia were very much in vogue in those days in some circles. Many of them greeted the invading German soldiers with flowers. This time there was no pretending on my part, Lonia knew me well: it was she who pretended she was not at all surprised to see me in the market in Kraków at a time when not a single Jew wearing an armband could be spotted on the streets of Kraków. We talked quite freely for a few minutes. She told me that she had been in touch with her employers who found themselves in Lwów, until the German invasion of Russia, when she lost contact with them. She was working as a clerk in the NSDAP. 'And how are you getting on?' she asked me. I do not remember my reply, it must have been rather non-committal. There was no mention of my present status as a person with no right to be at large. We said goodbye in the usual way, as if this had been an ordinary meeting. I thought about this meeting later and regretted not having tried to make further contact with her. Maybe she could

THE BEGINNING OF THE ROAD

have been useful in, for instance, obtaining documents or certificates. It was too late, I did not meet her again.

In the winter of 1941-2, we lived with the Krajewski family in Skawińska Street. This was in the vicinity of the Jewish hospital which was being liquidated at that time. The winter was hard and one day all the pipes burst. We were left with no water. A neighbour told me that there was a well near the hospital and all the tenants were going there to get water. I went there and the moment I passed the gate, I found myself face to face with a Jew wearing an armband. It was Emil, the same Emil who used to stand in the gate leading to the hospital and ensure that visitors would not outstay the visiting hours. Emil knew me well from the time at the beginning of 1940 when I had brought my father, who was gravely ill, to hospital for a skull trepanation. This had been after many trials and tribulations when, receiving the news from home about my father's illness, I went there immediately and brought him to Kraków, without a permit for rail travel and of course without the obligatory armband. Dr Grynberg, the nose and throat specialist at the Jewish hospital, told me when I asked him for permission to visit my father any time during the day to arrange it with Emil. I understood and during the two weeks of my father's stay in hospital, I was on very good terms with Emil. Now the Jewish hospital was being closed down, the remaining goods and equipment were being taken to the ghetto and Emil was probably supervising the move.

He must have recognised me even though I was dressed differently, in a sheepskin coat and a warm scarf on my head, because he asked in amazement, 'What are you doing here? '

I was a practised liar by that time so I answered without a moment's hesitation, 'I came here to get some water, apparently there is a well here.'

We stood opposite each other for a few seconds, I with the empty bucket in my hand, he with a look of bewilderment on his face.

'I think I know you,' he said at last.

I tried to smile, but I was not very successful. My lips were frozen and not just with cold. 'Of course,' I said at last, 'I often walk by here because I live nearby. May I get some water? '

'There.' He waved in the direction of a footpath trodden in the snow.

On my return with a bucketful of water, he was no longer there. But for the next few days I took the roundabout way to town. Then the hospital was locked, the pipes were mended, and there was no longer any need to go and fetch water. Was I afraid of the Jews? Indeed, I must admit I was. There were all sorts and we were often warned to be on our guard. For instance, Kłopotowski told me when sending me to Bochnia with the *'Kennkarten'* (identity cards) to be careful because two young Jews were on the prowl at the railway station, capturing Jews trying to make their escape. One had to live through such infamy.

After Cyrankiewicz's arrest the task of looking after us fell to Kłopotowski, as I have said, and he took it very seriously. He found us a flat in Skawińska Street with some people engaged in underground work, and he also found me legal employment. This job was arranged through Hanka Krajewska, the owner of our flat, and I was to be a gardener with a family living in the country near Kraków. It was not a live-in job, I usually went to work in the morning and would return to Kraków in the evening. It was a large villa with a huge, very beautiful garden. They had vegetable, fruit and flower gardens, all on a commercial scale. My childhood knowledge of gardening became an invaluable asset. Not one of the inhabitants of the house and least of all the housekeeper, suspected that a Jew would be able to plant cabbages with such expertise, to bed seedlings of onions, cauliflowers and other vegetables, to hill up potatoes and prune rose bushes in the conservatories. This job had several positive aspects. I did not need to go to work when Kłopotowski needed me in connection with conspiracy matters, because the owner of the house and the members of her large family knew that I was active in the underground. I used to bring them underground publications. Gardening itself was for me a respite and often saved me from despair. Sometimes I could imagine that time had stopped and I was tending my family's garden in Przybyszów. Strawberries grew in that garden too and the carrot and parsnip patches needed weeding. We had apple and pear trees and my mother, an expert gardener, would graft them with such skill that three kinds of fruit grew on one pear tree. In this large garden here, I could sometimes bury my face in the grass and cry without fear that someone would ask why I was crying.

THE BEGINNING OF THE ROAD

Actually, someone did ask me this question one day, but this was much later, in the summer of 1942, after my family had been removed to their deaths. My ability to hide my despair was failing me at that time. I noticed that people were looking at me with interest on tram journeys and it made me nervous: this was dangerous. Eventually one day the foster daughter of the owner of the villa with whom we were great friends, asked me directly 'Tell me, Marysia, are you Jewish?' It was a moment when I had to surrender, when the secret kept so long had become an unbearable burden. I said yes, and I could not hide my tears in Janka's small, cozy room. I was not afraid: I trusted this Polish girl completely. She did not disappoint me and she helped me at this very difficult time to place my small niece, miraculously saved from the Germans, in a convent near Kraków.

This garden work also had other advantages. I often used to stay the night there when Kraków or my current lodgings became particularly unsafe. Nobody was surprised when after a full day's work I would feel tired and would not feel like returning home for the night. Nobody tried to establish whether this was true or just a cover. On the practical side, apart from a small wage, I partook of all the garden produce and after Janka discovered I was Jewish, she always made sure I got my share of apples stored for winter for the family. An important asset for me was my official labour document, produced in my Aryan name by the Kraków *'Arbeitsamt'*, the German office dealing with these matters. This document saved me several times during street and train roundups to German labour camps. Finally, later, when I was working in the Council for Aid to the Jews (RPZ), I could arrange for financial help to Jewish families who were in hiding. This often happened in quite interesting circumstances. One of the families consisted of three people – mother, father and daughter, whose names I cannot remember. They were hiding in Janka's sister's flat in the Osiedle Oficerskie district, where most flats were occupied by the Germans. They spent two-and-a-half years behind a wardrobe and thus survived the war. A few people, who remained anonymous to me, were able to get aid through a friend of the family of my employers, a nun in the Ursuline Convent in Kraków. I kept the receipt signed by Sister Józefa for the money, which would this way reach our 'charges', as we called the Jews helped by the RPZ. My visits to the nun in the convent were further proof of my being Aryan: this noble old lady would express her approval and admiration for a Pole helping the Jews. One day she gave me a picture of the Holy Family and asked me to have it always by me. 'They will guard you in your dangerous work', she said. I carried this picture about with me, I somehow couldn't part with this gift from the heart. As it happened, this was the only evidence of my fraudulent identity, because I have never worn any cross or holy medal favoured by other Jews passing themselves off as Christians. I used to frequent churches quite regularly because it was a good place for couriers to meet.

An interesting instance of 'discovering' a Jewish family occurred in my place of work. One of the owner's grandsons, a youth of seventeen, loved music and himself played the piano beautifully. One day, going into the house from the garden for lunch, I heard from an open upstairs window the sounds of a Chopin mazurka, played with such brilliance that it was clear even to me with my limited musical knowledge that it was not Andrzejek who was playing. At lunch I met a Mr Nowak who, as I was informed, was visiting our neighbours. Later that day, when I was working in the garden, Andrzejek came up to me to tell me a secret: Mr Nowak who played so beautifully was no other than Jan Hofman, a famous Kraków pianist, a Jew, who was hiding in this village. For Andrzejek, a music lover, this disclosure was of no particular importance, he adored the brilliant interpreter of Chopin so much that he was not at all bothered by him being Jewish. But I thought it my duty to warn this young enthusiast. 'You must not', I said, 'put it about that he is Jewish. Surely you know why he is in hiding'. But even while issuing this warning, I had to admit that the organisation with which I had links could help people like Professor Hofman. I made no mention of what this organisation was or that it was helping Jews only. This is why Mr Hofman, when I met him at the flat of his Polish wife where his two sisters, Jula and Hanka, were hiding, was convinced that neither I nor the organisation for which I was working knew that he was Jewish. He thought I was helping him and his two sisters on a fairly regular basis (this meant not just providing them with money, but also with forged documents) on account of their having had to go into hiding for political reasons.

THE BEGINNING OF THE ROAD

This eventually led to a very interesting meeting after the war. In the first days of freedom I met Hofman accidentally in the street. He told me that he had just found a suitable flat in Chopin Street, but that he was without a penny and simply had no money to move and to furnish his new place. 'You know,' I said, 'I have got some money left from the aid funds. I shall try to find some money for you.'

He was greatly moved by this and decided to disclose his secret to me. 'I haven't told you this until now for reasons of security, but now I must tell you: I am Jewish.'

It was a very funny situation. I felt like laughing, but refrained from any mischievous comments. I said merely, 'I know, I have known all along. The aid you and your sisters were getting was meant solely and exclusively for Jews.'

In spite of his amazement and, I think, shock, at this revelation, he declared his willingness to repay the organisation which had such noble aims.

After the war when my being Jewish was no longer a secret, I met one day one of the sons of the owner of the villa in Michałowice who asked me if I could arrange for him and his family to get some decent flat in Kraków, 'Because you are the rulers here now'. This comment was not without good reason and later turned out to be tragic in its consequences. But it did not apply to me and I had to explain it to this gentleman: I was homeless myself at that time.

I met Andrzejek, the music lover, at Professor Hofman's first public concert after the war. He brought an enormous bouquet of flowers and a great deal of emotion. For him Chopin and Hofman were one.

MORDECAI

The places where we stayed make quite a story. We were seldom both registered in the same flat, anyway we tried not to live where we were registered. Our peregrinations can be reconstructed from the *Kennkarten* which we have kept until this day.

Our first official registration using my *Kennkart* was at Kommandaturstr. 17, i.e. Stradom Street. The date can no longer be deciphered, but it was in the beginning of 1941 when Jews were already confined to the ghetto, i.e. at a time when

Kraków was *'Judenrein'*. Many odd things which we have not fathomed until now were taking place in connection with this flat. The sitting tenant there was a young Jewess, the daughter of Marysia's pre-war friends, the Sternfelds. In the summer of 1939 she married a Jew from Kowno. They got separated by the war, but he sent her a Lithuanian passport which entitled her to live outside the ghetto. She was not obliged to wear the armband and she received German food coupons. She was young and pretty, with very semitic looks. It was not a good idea to appear with her in the street, because the police, particularly the Polish police, would immediately check her identity papers. They recognised such Jewish beauty much better than the Germans.

It was only much later that we discovered how dangerous this flat was. We owe it to our extreme good fortune and to the strange instinct which often saved us that we were not then captured by the Gestapo. Our landlady had the best of intentions, she offered us shelter at a time when we had no roof over our heads, but she was over-confident and very thoughtless. Every day, particularly in the evenings, young people – Jews on forged documents and Poles working in the underground – would gather in her flat. A Marian Jodłowski was a frequent visitor there; as it later turned out he was a Gestapo informer and was liquidated by the Polish underground in October 1944. Luckily, I had worked it out much earlier and on the basis of many observations, and particularly his behaviour on our way to Lwów when he insisted on accompanying me, deduced that we must leave the flat immediately. I managed to convince Marysia who had also been questioned by him that we had to do it. He knew about our connections with the socialist underground and kept trying to get information from us about 'Teodor' – Adam Rysiewicz – a very active member of the underground. Maybe his attempts to penetrate the underground cell of the Polish Socialist Party with our help saved us from early arrest. We left the flat in time. But of the group of young people who used to visit, a few were captured by the Gestapo, among them a young Pole, Bronek Sasula.

The next registration on my *Kennkart* of 4 April 1942 bore the address 'Alten Weichselstrasse 64, flat 16' – it was the German name of Starowiślna Street, translated literally. I lived there on and off for over a year until the moment when Bojko, a Ukrainian policeman with the German force, started to pursue me. I was not suspected of being a Jew, but of helping the Jews, not that the consequences of my arrest would have been any different. But, again, I managed to avoid arrest.

My last accommodation registration under the Germans was of October 1943 at 32 Zielna Street in the Dębniki district of Kraków. Marysia had been registered there from July 1942. My registration was forged. I was neither in the registration book of the house nor in the police records but in case of an 'ordinary' identity check, I could say that I was an inhabitant of a specific street in Kraków, and not a homeless, hunted creature. 'Edyś', a worker in the organisation RPZ, was a brilliant forger of names, stamps and all other accessories of underground life.

At that time, Marysia and I used to live sometimes together, but more often not. When one place became unsafe, we had to look for something new, even if just for one night. We had a few places to choose from. One was a flat in Bocheńska Street which was in the Jewish quarter, except the Jews were no longer there. We had business connections with the owner of the flat, Janiczek, who was our main bread dealer. This bread, obtained on forged food coupons and sold on the black market, was our main source of revenue, together with thousands of cigarettes taken secretly from a 'Germans only' shop. For transporting a suitcase containing a thousand cigarettes and delivering it at a given address, we would get a hundred for ourselves.

Let no-one think that to carry such a suitcase through the streets patrolled all day in the most unexpected places by policemen, both German and Polish, was child's play. The Polish policemen could at least be bribed with cigarettes – or so we were told – but happily the occasion for bribery did not arise. We became experienced in avoiding danger. I used to choose the busiest main streets, and look the Germans and other suspicious characters I passed straight in the eye. I tried not to look as if I was carrying something heavy, but to step lightly and with ease. But I must admit that all this psychological approach would have been worth absolutely nothing if it had not been for the little bit of luck which had not deserted me. This also applied to situations much more dangerous than the cigarette one.

But I have digressed from our place at the Janiczkis' and our trade in bread. The food coupons printed in the underground the night after the official ones appeared, must have been Kłopotowski's idea, the result of his inventiveness and initiative. The colour of the official coupons was changed every month, but the underground printers must have had large supplies of printing-ink in different colours, because at first glance it was difficult to tell the real coupons from the forged ones. Maybe a detailed, systematic study would have brought this blessed forgery to light, but the coupons we used were never studied in this way.

The bread sold by our 'agent', Janiczek, was bought by regular customers among the peasants of Podhale in the Tatra mountains. This part of Poland, which had the least farm land, had a bread shortage even before the war and even more so now, when the Germans were confiscating the tiny amount of grain that grew there.

The Janiczkis' flat consisted of one large room and a small kitchen. In this one room a narrow, iron bed would be put up for us for the night. But I must say that these simple people must have had quite a feeling of community with the homeless like ourselves. I do not know whether they suspected we were Jewish, probably not, but even just allowing non-registered people to stay the night could arouse the neighbours' and, most important, the concierge's suspicions. The concierge was an important representative of the authorities in those days. Early one morning, when Mrs Janiczek had just returned home having completed the first commercial 'operation', we heard her, while still half asleep, say to her husband: 'This Koziol has been moaning and groaning again about our putting up some unregistered people here and that we don't know how it might end.' Janiczek grumbled something non-committal in reply, but we both understood the meaning of this remark. We had not quite abandoned this refuge, but we tried only to use it when it came to the worst.

My friendship with Janiczek was on a man-to-man basis. I was his confidant in matters of the heart. This tall, bony man, an almost illiterate gas company worker who used to down five litres of soup for dinner from an enormous bowl (we used to watch him, fascinated), was in fact a tender troubadour, madly in love with some beauty three times the size of his own wife,

THE BEGINNING OF THE ROAD

who was as thin as a rake. I had to mediate between the quarrelling spouses. Mrs Janiczek had to be assured that this was just a phase and that he would get over it, and he had to be dissuaded from the dangerous decision to leave his wife and home. These were not trivial matters, unrelated to our own fate. Each such quarrel, heard throughout the house, attracted attention unnecessary to the rowing couple and its suspect tenants. Thus often, very often, everyday domestic trivia had a bearing on our lives, sometimes positive and sometimes negative.

Zygmunt Kłopotowski was, until his arrest (in the spring of 1943, if memory serves me right), our leader and our attentive and responsible guardian. Naturally, we were not told about his rank in the Polish underground, but his involvement with helping the Jews certainly sprang from his human and personal attitude and not from orders by the Polish underground. We now learn from books and documents published after the war that he was the head of counter-intelligence of the Union for the Armed Struggle (Związek Walki Zbrojnej) for the Kraków region. This explains some of his master strokes which we admired so much. His various connections in all sorts of circles – from factory workers to university professors, from blackmarket traders to totally devoted underground workers – gave him great scope for action. It was an underground network which must have been very intricate and dangerous because it proved in the end to be very treacherous. His arrest was a great personal blow to us, and not just to us: many Jewish matters which he embarked on remained unresolved.

We were his couriers in Jewish matters. It was the period long before the emergence of the official organisation of aid to the Jews (RPZ 'Żegota'), and the hardest time of Nazi operations and transports to death camps. Kłopotowski had numerous Jewish friends and acquaintances. He would arrange Aryan documents for them, forged by a military 'legalisation' cell, and this was no easy thing because the attitude of these organisations was mostly unfriendly and, at best, indifferent to the fate of the Jews. How he managed to convince them and to what extent he took advantage of his position in the underground when the photograph to be used on the *Kennkart* did not look altogether gentile, has remained his secret. I only know that he would look carefully at each photo I brought him and comment on it in his own way. For instance, 'Oh, this must be a very pretty girl. A bit too pretty, she will turn heads which is not a good thing. And what colour are her eyes? You are very keen on her, I'm sure, but how will she look on a German *Kennkart*, that is the question . . .'. He never refused help, however, and not just in the matter of documents. He often tried to find people a place to live. This was a difficult task and we often helped him.

2

ON THE KRAKÓW-TARNÓW-LWÓW LINE

MORDECAI

At this time, in the summer of 1941, Jews started to return to Tarnów, particularly the young ones, who up till then had lived on the Soviet side. They realised very soon that this had been a perilous idea. The family instinct inherent in the Jews led these people to return to their homes, parents, children, to their own people. Death awaited them. The German police, the Polish police, all sorts of agents, secret agents and other collaborators were rounding up the arriving Jews so that some of them never even had a chance of crossing the threshold of their longed-for homes. My brother Juda died in this way. He lived on 'the other side' in a village near Sambor. His wife, a doctor in the Jewish hospital at Tarnów, had stayed with her family. Juda returned to be with her at last. I do not even know the circumstances of his arrest – he was executed with others who had returned. He was not survived for long by his wife, Sianka Schaechter, who was shot with a group of Jewish doctors during one of the 'special operations'.

The German invasion of the territories occupied by the Soviets changed not only the war situation, but also my personal one. Political subjects are the domain of historians, my subject is people, Jews, my brothers and sisters, because in each of them I saw my family, my big, wretched family, melting away.

My escapades eastwards were of a different nature now. I was in the service of friends who had relatives on the other side. I was Zygmunt Kłopotowski's courier. At that time – and for a long time – there was no official organisation for helping the Jews. But he was himself such an organisation. Quiet, calm, full of ideas, and above all, a devoted friend of the Jews. He valued my courage, he believed in my lucky stars; he continually added to my responsibilities, but he himself did not shrink from the most difficult tasks in helping the Jews. It was a sideline to his main activities, after all, he was a key figure in the Polish underground. We did not know at the time what his exact role in the underground organisation was, but we could guess that it was something very important.

Not long after the Germans invaded Lwów in the summer of 1941, I went from Tarnów to Żółkiew at the request of Cesia Holzer. She had a brother there, a young boy who was staying with a Polish family under the Soviets. He was working and, worse still, belonged to the Komsomol. His family in Tarnów had received letters from him until the outbreak of the German-Soviet war; now all contact was lost.

I received the exact address of the Poles with whom he was staying and I called on them. The parents and their daughter were at home. I introduced myself by my Aryan name. In their eyes I was a Pole, of course. I explained that I came at the request of a friend of mine, to find out what had happened to her brother. They told me that eight days earlier the Germans had taken away their four sons together with a fifth, a Jew who had stayed with them the entire time of the Soviet occupation. From that moment they had had no news about their fate: they were not in the local prison.

It was the summer of 1941, after the first pogroms in Żółkiew. As in all other large and small towns of Eastern Galicia, the Ukrainians with the Germans' blessing were 'settling their accounts' with the Jews. Jews were constantly being thrown out of their homes; being robbed and murdered continually. The Germans tried on their arrival in Żółkiew to destroy an ancient synagogue built like a fortress centuries before. They did not succeed, not even with the use of dynamite, but they set fire to the interior and the building stood like a grim skeleton, visible from afar, like an ominous warning to all those Jews who lived on the remainders of hope, a typically Jewish hope, that maybe it would not be so bad after all . . . .

In Żółkiew at that time I had one of my strangest experiences. I lived through many strange experiences under occupation, but this one was exceptional: the parents of the arrested boys suggested that I should visit a certain Jewish lad called

ON THE KRAKÓW-TARNÓW-LWÓW LINE

Schlosser who was considered in Żółkiew to be a clairvoyant. Apparently, the Polish police had used him before the war to solve various crimes. My hosts' daughter went with me. We found this Schlosser in a small room – a young man, white as a sheet, he sat there and looked at us without a word. I told him that I had come a long way and that I was begging him for help. I explained what it was about. The girl, whom he knew, told him how eight days before the Germans took away her four brothers and another boy, a Jew who was staying with them. Where were they? I put ten złotys on the table. He pushed the money away. He looked at me: we looked in each other's eyes. After a moment he seemed to have fallen asleep for a few minutes. When he woke up, he was trembling all over. He said that the four would return home, but that the fifth one was dead.

We returned with this news to the Poles' home. I stayed the night there. The following day their four sons returned home. Young Holzer had been taken separately by the Germans on their first day and nobody saw him again. But they had heard that he had been shot dead on the spot. This was all I could tell his family in Tarnów. I handed them a small bundle containing his clothes, all that was left of a handsome young boy. It was a hard mission – not the first one and not the last.

All that happened around us in those days was a matter of chance, even when we had plans worked out for the following day. How could one foresee what would happen after going into the street, crossing the road and entering the house where one had an appointment, or who would open the door when one rang the bell or knocked in the agreed manner? It might happen that the Germans or some stooges in their service had set up a trap in this flat to round up as many people from the underground as possible.

The events registered in the notes left from the time of occupation, scraps of paper preserved with difficulty, taken from place to place – cannot always be reconstructed today. These are sometimes names or just first names of people whose faces are lost to memory. There are also dates of events, probably important and interesting, but what they were has been forgotten. There are also days and nights which have remained for ever engraved in the memory.

WITNESSES

When we lived together, we said goodbye each day – silently – as if for ever. The words 'see you' were like a blessing. The route of my journeys from Kraków to Lwów included two particularly dangerous railway stations, Tarnów and Przemyśl. In Tarnów, where I lived for the greatest part of my life, any informant would have recognised me within a few minutes, and there were many of them about, particularly at the railway stations. If this happened, neither my forged documents nor my Aryan looks, nor even the supposed, non-existent, Argentinian passport would have been of any use to me. Again, it was thanks to my lucky stars that nothing untoward ever happened to me on my innumerable trips. In Przemyśl the train stopped for long enough to enable the Germans to make a search. One such night search has stayed in my memory in particular.

I was taught by experience – an idea, maybe illusory, possibly dictated by instinct – that it was safer by night. This particular night it became evident just how illusory it was. The train had no light. We sat in a compartment, six men, not able to see even each other's faces, when I was suddenly woken up from my nap by the fierce light of an electric lamp. Without thinking I shouted furiously, 'What the hell is going on?' A shaft of light was directed at me and at the same time a hoarse German voice repeated furiously, 'What the hell, what the hell', followed by a characteristic 'Komm mit', to all my travelling companions, but not to me. This time the train stayed in Przemyśl for a few hours.

At dawn, four passengers returned to the compartment, the fifth one was missing. 'What was it? ' I asked. 'What happened to the other one?'

'Well, they rounded up a group of men and told us to drop our trousers. They picked a few yids, also the one who was sitting with us here, and bumped them off on the spot, by the railway track.'

Silence, no comments. Before the train started, a 'Black' Ukrainian (*Bahnschutz*) came into our compartment and ordered us to show him the luggage of the boy who was 'bumped off' by the railway track. He took away his suitcase. The train moved off.

In the first years of the war, many Jews settled in Tarnów, entire families driven off from the western parts of Poland; especially from Bielsko and Katowice. I befriended the

ON THE KRAKÓW-TARNÓW-LWÓW LINE

Birnbaum family from Bielsko. The father was a chemist: he got a job in a jam factory. They had a very pretty daughter, Litka. I wanted to save her, and I brought her to Kraków together with her mother. But it was not successful, even though I arranged with Kłopotowski's help for the mother to get Aryan documents and somewhere to stay. Litka had a friend in Kraków, a music teacher who used to give her lessons before the war. The trust she had in this Mr G. and his wife turned out to be misplaced, to such an extent that it nearly ended in my arrest. Litka and her mother came back to Tarnów after some very dramatic experiences and perished, possibly in Bełżec. The fate of this family has left a deep impression in my heart. I find it difficult, even today, to think and talk about it. But I shall return to this story later on.

For the moment, it was still September 1941. I was again on my way to Lwów, again in the service of friends, these same Birnbaums. Julian Grubner, Mrs Birnbaum's brother, fled to Lwów after being expelled from Bielsko. There, during the Soviet occupation, he worked as an accountant in a furniture factory in Zielona Street. He was a widower with two daughters and he lost his job when the Germans entered Lwów and had nothing to live on. I visited him there a few times, bringing him food from his sister and finally, as he said, bringing him luck, because on my third visit, I found him promoted to chief accountant in the same factory as before. The Germans took over the firm which was called Niesel und Kämmer, and produced office and hotel furniture and other wood products. The head office of this firm was in Berlin. This was a stroke of luck not just for the Jew Grubner, but also for me. Through the good offices of Grubner, who had earned the complete trust of the factory's directors, I received a dream of a document, the best for those times, in my Aryan name, with stamps, signatures, with the German 'crow', i.e. the eagle with a swastika, and even with 'Heil Hitler'. Here is the approximate translation of this *Ausweis*, or pass, dated 1 July 1942

It is hereby certified that the Pole, Mieczysław Józef Piotrowski, born in 1908 in Rokitno, domiciled in Kraków, 64 Starowiślna Street, is employed in the Kraków district and Galicia as the buyer of hardware such as nails, belts, etc., needed in great quantities in our factory.

WITNESSES

It is requested that Mr Piotrowski be allowed to fulfil his duties without impediment.

In addition, on 11 January 1943, I received a work certificate (*Beschäftingungs-Ausweis*) from the official military officer in Lwów (*Heeresbauamt Lemberg, Bauleitung Lemberg*) with my photograph and every conceivable stamp. On the reverse of this document are the dates of its renewals. The last one was 31 December 1943. At that time there were no Jewish prisoners left in the Janów Camp, and Lwów was *Judenrein*. The Jews who were still alive were hiding in bunkers and other places: a handful of them survived. My travels to Lwów ended, but before this happened, I went there several times.

Regarding the documents I have kept until this day and which I quote here, I must stress that I have not got on my conscience a single nail purchased for the factory Niesel und Kämmer. These documents served one purpose only: to help and to save, to watch and to remember. I had a smile on my lips and bitterness in my heart: a smile which was my defence against suspicion and treachery, bitterness and despair at the sight of what was happening around me. I felt no fear for myself, for my own life, my own safety. I was condemned to this kind of life and I accepted my fate in full consciousness.

It is difficult to explain what the supervision of the technical staff was like in this factory if not one of its directors took an interest in what I was doing there. They all knew me and one of them, Fannenstein, was particularly fond of me. The German managers employed there were: Köller, Hering, Fraulein Klier, plus five Ukrainian clerks, one half-Pole, half-Ukrainian who was a buyer for the firm in the Lwów area, and Holub, the Ukrainian driver. The Germans were simply draft dodgers and they tried to work efficiently because they did not want to be sent to the front line. This man Fannenstein, an ex-officer, had lost a leg in the war and had an artificial one. In addition to his job in the factory, he had his own business, a soda-water factory. One day he offered me the job of manager in his business and insisted that I go and see the factory. I could not get out of it. I thought I recognised a familiar face among the men and women working there. Yes, it came to me later, it was a Pole from Tarnów; we had gone to school together.

I did not have to wait long for the results of this visit. The following day, Grubner told me that Fannenstein wanted to have a word with me at the office, in private, and he warned me that someone had betrayed me and reported that I was Jewish. I thought about it, but only for a moment. Not to go to this meeting would have meant to abandon all my contacts and connections, and having to leave Lwów. No, I couldn't do it, I had to take that risk. This Fannenstein did not seem dangerous to me, he was doing good business in Lwów, surely not all of it strictly legal, so he would not be too keen to involve the Gestapo. Such was my very logical thinking, but . . . I put a question mark after 'but' and went to see him.

Fannenstein did not beat about the bush. He told me direct that someone had informed him that I was a Jew, but that to him it was of no consequence. I could become a manager in his firm and he would make sure I was safe.

I kept my *sang froid*. It is hard for me today to describe how I felt. There were moments when the tension made one hard and ready for anything. I had to react quickly, everything depended on my reaction: not just my own safety but the fate of very many people. I was not naive enough to rely on what this German said, even if he was a 'good' German. He was good for himself, for his own interests. He had one aim only: to seize a chance and to make as much money as possible. He would look after my safety as long as it was convenient for him. If the situation changed, if it meant endangering his own life, he would care about me exactly as much as about any other Jew. In the event, he did not even save Grubner of whom he thought so highly and was so fond.

I decided to assume yet another role, quite different from those I had been playing until this moment. I had only a few seconds to think about it. I said, 'You have been misinformed, I am not a Jew. But if this information reaches anyone who takes an interest in such matters, I would be just as much in danger. They could then find out that I am an ex-field officer and that I had not come forward to be registered when such an order was issued. It will be better for both of us if I do not accept this post.'

I could see the effect of this 'revelation' on Fannenstein. One of his eyelids started to twitch nervously, but he managed to control himself, said a few casual words and said goodbye as if nothing had happened. From this moment, however, he clearly avoided me and I did not seek his company either. He did turn out to be a decent German, that is, for his own safety and security he had left me in peace too. It was all I wanted from him.

I had friends in this factory. Even if it sounds funny, I was popular there with Poles and Ukrainians. One of the workers, a Pole and a patriot, had bared his soul to me and I trusted him, and in the eighteen months of my escapades to Lwów, I used to bring him the Polish underground press.

The Ukrainian driver used to get from me for further resale all kinds of goods such as saccharine, sugar, cigarette lighters – all things which were in short supply in Lwów. I sold them to him at cost so he made good money from this trade and he was totally devoted to me. I myself often obtained money for my journey to Lwów only with the greatest difficulty, but all this was not about making money.

The Ukrainian guards standing at the gate received various rations. This was arranged with the Germans by Grubner, but he asked me to distribute the rations and those who received them thought I had arranged it. All this created a particular atmosphere.

I had never lived in a hotel, I had my own room in the factory's offices at 204 Zielona Street. On the second floor in the same building lived a Polish family. The father, a carpenter, worked in the factory. All he ever read was the Bible, particularly the Old Testament. I think he may have been a Seventh Day Adventist. His son, Staszek, also worked in the factory, but then I lost sight of him. He kept going away; I was convinced that he was doing some business on the side. The Poles had learned to trade by then and it seemed they were better at it than the Jews.

At last one day I found Staszek at home. He was very smartly dressed. He boasted about various things he had bought and showed me presents for his parents and sisters.

'Well, Staszek,' I said, 'have you found yourself a rich widow?'

'I know better than to get married,' he replied, 'but you can make some money, too, if you want to. Come to Lublin with me. I walk the streets there and look around and I have yet to be wrong. I can tell a Jew or Jewess at first sight. I call them aside and take whatever they have got on them. And if they haven't got anything, I take them straight to the police station. For this I get paid, too. Come with me, you won't regret it.'

It was an effort not to punch him in the face. I turned to his father, the assiduous Bible reader,

'What do you think about what your son is doing, denouncing people to their death?'

The old man was neither indignant nor embarrassed. 'Mr Piotrowski,' he said, 'but it clearly says here in the Old Testament that the Jews must perish for their sins! The Jewish prophets themselves have said it!'

Where are you, the sages of Israel, creators of the great Book written to make the world a better place? Did you not foresee that by humbling yourselves before God and admitting your sins, you signed a death warrant on your sons and grandsons up to the hundredth generation? Did you not foresee that this Book would fall into the hands of barbarians who would take it upon themselves to carry out God's sentence?

Then came 1942, a year which did away with any remaining hope or illusions. There were no longer individual round-ups, isolated murders, draconian decrees and persecutions. As the 'actions' (this innocuous name meant in reality the deportations of Jews to death camps) intensified, so the number of Kłopotowski's clients and mine grew. Kłopotowski, as I have mentioned, had many Jewish friends. One such family he put under my care. Their real name was Mandel; before the war they had a draper's shop in Kraków. After their resettlement from Kraków to some small town, they lost their only child, a boy, in one of the first 'actions'. Broken by this tragedy, they returned to Kraków and got in touch with Zygmunt. He found them a flat and supplied them with Aryan papers in the name of 'Lorek'. Being registered, they did not need to be in hiding, yet they felt most insecure. Kłopotowski asked me to visit them as often as possible, because in the eyes of their landlords, visits from a gentile such as me would count for more than the possession of Aryan documents. They believed unreservedly that I was a gentile and when I tried to comfort them in their unhappiness, they would say, 'We know you are a decent Pole and have real sympathy for us, but how can you understand our pain?' How ironic that remark was! I, a 'gentile' seeing my people, my family, my dearest friends, perish day by day, had to bite my tongue to stop myself from telling them the truth. All day long they played solitaire, wept and talked of suicide. There was something tragi-comic in how they kept planning which one of them should commit suicide by poisoning – they had decided that one of them should stay alive.

Instead of giving them the poison, I offered to find the husband, as the one who was in greater danger, something to do in 'my' factory in Lwów. Grubner, a brave man and devoted to me, assured me of his help. Kłopotowski agreed to my plan and we both managed to persuade Lorek that this would be safer for them both. As a woman his wife had a better chance of survival alone.

I got him a work permit and registration at the address of a Ukrainian working in the factory. I sent him to Lwów in the company of Bolek Krajewski, a Pole who was a friend of Kłopotowski. Marysia was registered at the Krajewskis' place in Skawińska Street and we both lived there until the summer of 1942, Marysia legally and I without registration.

This Bolek was quite a character, a boozer and a decent chap. Before the war he had worked as a pastry chef on the ship *Batory* and he could produce wonderful confectionery concoctions even from such humble ingredients as were available on the food coupons. He also had the characteristic gait of a sailor, swaying slightly when he walked, which was often the result of too much booze. He also had a drunken bravado, he was not afraid of the Germans, and it was only by luck that he had not brought on us some disaster.

Bolek's wife, Hanka, was very active in the underground. She kept a duplicating machine which, in addition to the two of us, was quite enough incriminating evidence for one flat.

Lorek's journey to Lwów with Krajewski was uneventful. Bolek described it to us in some detail: Mandel/Lorek, being a specialist in textiles by profession, took great interest in how his travelling companions were dressed and pronounced expert verdicts on the quality of materials from which their clothes were made. Bolek acted out the conversation with black humour for us.

The entire venture did not go according to plan. Lorek, in spite of good Polish documents and fairly good Polish looks, was too nervous to show up at the factory and after a while went back to Kraków. This time he travelled alone and, luckily,

ON THE KRAKÓW-TARNÓW-LWÓW LINE

without incident. He claimed that the Ukrainian with whom he was staying in Lwów frightened him by saying that some suspicious character was asking about him. This was enough for Lorek to pack his suitcase and depart in great haste.

Shortly afterwards I found myself in Lwów again and this is what I heard:

'Mr Piotrowski', the Ukrainian with whom Lorek was staying said to me, 'what has got into you, sending me this yid to stay here?'

I feigned surprise and outrage, but to no avail.

'This guy was shouting in his sleep and talking Yiddish! So I gave him a little fright and he took himself off. I am not going to keep a Jew here, after all!'

I had no other choice, but to agree with him and pretend that I had also been taken in by this man, that I had no idea that he was a Jew. What a nerve! This insolent Jew had dreamt at night his horrendous Jewish dreams and kept reproaching his Jewish God for taking away his only child. In what language could he quarrel with God if not in Yiddish? But this could have been his undoing. However, Mandel was lucky this time too. Nobody suspected me of anything and he survived the occupation. Kłopotowski found the couple another flat, gave them new documents, this time in the name of 'Migdal'. Mrs Migdal died soon after the war; her heart, the heart of a mother, was obviously not strong enough. We met Mandel with his new wife and small son in Paris in 1948 from where they went on to Canada, and we lost touch with them. I hope that he no longer suffers from nightmares, that life has proved stronger than tragedy.

Each of my journeys to Lwów was in those times – 1942 – punctuated by continuous 'operations'. Grubner, who stayed in his position of chief accountant of the Niesel und Kämmer firm until the final liquidation of the Janówski Camp, kept us informed about each new action. Each left thousands of Jews murdered on the spot, in the streets and at the 'sands' next to the Janówski Camp. Also, tens of thousands of people were being sent to their death in Bełżec.

The factory where Monek Ortzman worked had a branch at Zamarstynowska Street. He was an old friend from Tarnów and a reserve officer in the Polish Army before the war. At my request, Grubner brought him to our office. I offered to get him identity papers and to arrange for his move to Kraków. I was hoping to be able, with Kłopotowski's help, to get him fixed up somehow, but he refused to go without his wife. This is where most of the problems in saving people arose. It was understandable that families did not want to be separated and would rather die together – parents with children, sister with 'good Polish looks' along with brothers, who were always more in danger simply because they were men. I offered to meet Monek in three days' time and to bring him weapons so that he could escape, save himself in time. But he refused. He said that taking weapons to an extermination camp would not change anything, that it would only endanger everybody around him, and that he was not ready to escape. I could see that he was simply afraid. Nobody could be saved by force. Only someone determined, ready for anything, aware that death at the hands of the Germans was inevitable and that his only chance to save himself was by escaping, only such a risk taker had a chance of survival. And there were people who, without any special contacts, without plans, without any immediate help, staked their all and won their lives. There are statistics of those who were successful, but those who perished in such attempts can never be counted.

One such fugitive whom I came across in Kraków was a friend from Tarnów, called Nisan Feuer. I met him quite by chance at the entrance to the Roman Baths in Kraków. His reaction to seeing me was most original: he clapped his hands and shouted, luckily not very loud, 'I shall live! I shall live!' I watched him in amazement. He told me that he had escaped deportation from Tarnów, that he had no documents and was looking for me because he had heard from various friends in Tarnów that I was helping the Jews. He had told himself that if he met me, he would survive the war. Before he met me, he found shelter in Borek Fałęcki on the outskirts of Kraków, with a lonely Polish widow whom he knew from the times when he used to trade in forests. She owned a large farm near Tuchów at that time. At one point, when they were both young, they had been quite intimate, or at least so he was hinting. But now, despite fond memories, she would not allow him to stay with her without documents. I got him papers in the name of Jan Kasprzycki and I visited him from time to time, as I did other similar 'gentiles'. My visits were to show his benefactress that he had Polish friends in an underground organisation.

Kasprzycki had good Aryan looks. He was tall and well built, he wore a hat with a green feather like German civilians did and he really looked like a German. He confided in me about his love affairs and I mention this here because they were so typical in those days. I think that such personal adventures illustrate a side of life not written about by historians. But these are human matters around which the double life of the 'paper' Jews evolved.

This Kasprzycki, a virile man in his prime, was looking for some physical release – to put it delicately – and through an advertisement in a Kraków newspaper he met a woman who, as she put it in the advertisement, was looking for a male companion with whom 'to share pleasant moments'. It seemed there was nothing simpler: two lonely people were looking for company. They met and they liked each other. But here Kasprzycki's tragedy started. This woman was obviously eagerly looking for love and the conditions were very propitious: Kasprzycki was keen on her and she had her own flat. But Kasprzycki remembered that he was not Kasprzycki, that his real name was Feuer, and he had a sudden attack of fear that his cover would be blown. This tragedy was not as funny as it might seem. Kasprzycki came to me for advice. I could help him and I did help him in other matters, but this one, I felt, exceeded my competence. He showed me the love letters which this woman wrote to him at his *poste restante* address and this was as far as the poor man had got with her.

With Teodor's help, we despatched this Kasprzycki to Hungary at the end of 1943 and a few months later I met him in Budapest. He was extremely grateful for my help and he solemnly declared that after the war he would polish my shoes every day. But this act of gratitude never materialised because he left for America and I have not heard from him since.

One more interesting detail has stayed in my memory, something Marysia told me after the war. It was she who had prepared Feuer for his departure to Hungary and he had not suspected even for a moment that she was Jewish herself. From Hungary he returned direct to Kraków after the war and like all the other survivors, he turned up one day in the Jewish Committee at Długa Street. Marysia worked there in the children's welfare department. He greeted her with great joy and praised the Committee for employing such 'a noble Pole' who was helping the Jews!

Among my various Lwów experiences, one has remained a mystery until this day. I was approached one day by a German working as a clerk in our factory, a Miss Klier, who asked me to go with her to her flat and help her transport some things she needed. I had no reason to think up some excuse. We knew each other well and we often talked. But this time, as at other times, I followed some kind of instinct. I told Holub, the driver who, as I have said, was a decent chap, to wait for me, that I would be back in a minute. I said it to him in Polish as I sat next to him during our ride to Miss Klier's flat.

It was five o'clock in the afternoon. We arrived in front of the house where she lived on the second floor. I helped her to carry some small items upstairs and thought that she could have done it herself as there was nothing there which was heavy. This fact alone put me on guard. She showed me her new flat and asked me to stay to tea. I refused politely saying that the driver was waiting for me and would get impatient. 'The driver is not waiting,' she said with great certainty, 'I told him to go back to the factory'. I was sure that he was waiting; I glanced through the window and indeed he was. She looked through the window too and I could see that she was furious. But I did not wait for her reaction, I said goodbye and ran downstairs. On my way out I was stopped by a tall, powerfully built man in civilian clothes and boots, a typical German. He asked me if Miss Klier lived here. 'Yes,' I told him, 'on the second floor'. Holub had started the engine, I got into the car and we left.

At night, when I was lying sleeplessly in my bed, I started thinking about it all. I had the worrying feeling that I had met this German before. Even more worrying was the feeling of anxiety which would not leave me. Whenever I did get an attack of anxiety, I tried to find the reasons for it, it was my instinct warning me of danger. Finally I fell asleep but not for long. I remembered where I had met the German, I had seen him a few times in the office in a Gestapo uniform when he came to settle some accounts for furniture made by the factory for the Gestapo. So Miss Klier had set up a trap for me, but why? I was trying to find some logical explanation for it and I have been trying to find one until this day. Maybe she wanted to blow my cover with the aid of this Gestapo man and without creating a scandal at the office? My position at the office was very strong: maybe she wanted to blackmail me? Maybe she thought I had money and would want to pay for her silence? Anyway, she had not frightened me and made no more similar attempts. And the whole thing has remained an unsolved mystery until this day, another of the mysteries of the fate which led me through 'fire and flood'.

3
WE BORE WITNESS

MORDECAI

June 1942: We had no direct contact with the Kraków ghetto. We had no choice but to avoid the 'Jewish quarter' which was understandable behaviour for supposed Aryans. But on the eve of the first, large-scale resettlement, we learned what was to happen. It was a hot, beautiful day. I do not remember the exact date, but it was the beginning of the month. We had a day off, we were not expected anywhere so we decided to pretend we were ordinary folk and we went to the beach on the Vistula River. We took with us Hanka Krajewska's much loved dog. This was also part of the camouflage, to make us look more convincing gentiles. We knew of many cases of Jews who had Aryan papers and were not in hiding, but walked the streets apparently freely, arming themselves with such additional evidence. A man walking his dog looked normal. It was best if the dog could be a mongrel. Heaven forbid it should be an Alsatian: an Alsatian was a German attribute.

Three Germans came and lay next to us on the beach. They must have had a day off too. They spoke quite loudly so we could hear when they talked about some *Sonderaktion* on the next day. They must have got a day's leave before this 'special action'.

The following day we knew what job awaited them. The Kraków ghetto had been surrounded. It was the first 'resettlement' to the death camp in Bełżec. But nobody knew about this camp yet, at least nothing certain – there was talk of labour camps somewhere in the Ukraine. It was months before the terrible truth reached us. Rumours about the way people were being killed abounded, each more horrible than the last. The

Jews whose relatives had been in those first transports paid all the money they had left to Polish and German railwaymen, in the hope that they would see their relatives and bring back some sign of life. Some of these people were crooks who preyed on such tragedies.

Kłopotowski had a lot of work for us. He was looking for accommodation, hiding places, if only temporary, for a few days, before something better and safer could be found. We were messengers of hope, which was frail and uncertain in this world of crime and baseness. We were constantly on the move, within a 'chalk circle', condemned to such a life by the strength of imagination of this man who was our 'boss', our friend and an untiring friend of the Jews.

A few days after the liquidation of the Kraków ghetto, Marysia and I went to Tarnów, not knowing that we would witness the first resettlement of the Tarnów Jews. Marysia wanted to go to see her people who, having been resettled from their farm in Przybyszów, were living at the time in the small town of Pilzno. She had tried desperately to persuade her parents, sister and brother-in-law and their daughters to escape. She had not been successful. Like most of the Jewish families, they did not want to be parted and it was impossible for six people to escape together. She hoped to be able to persuade them this time at least to have their photographs ready for the *Kennkarten*. Neither of us realised how little time there was left before the handful of Jews still living in Pilzno would be liquidated.

We parted at the Tarnów railway station – Marysia was to find out what was happening to my family – it was not possible for me to appear in Panna Maria Street where I was well known. Even my excellent document and Aryan features would not have saved me there if I was spotted by a police spy or an ad hoc informer. I promised Grubner that I would find out how the Birnbaum family were getting on. Marysia and I arranged to meet at the railway station in the afternoon.

We discovered very quickly what the situation was like in Tarnów, at the exit from the station. We came across a column of Jews led to a rallying point from where they were put into railway carriages. We did not know that a massacre was taking place in the town, that people were being dragged from their homes and shot dead on the spot, that they were being segregated on the market place and those unable to travel were being taken by lorries to the Jewish cemetery and to Zblitowska Góra where graves were ready for those under sentence of death: children, the old and the infirm.

I do not know, I cannot explain why we did not turn back immediately and take the next train back to Kraków. It was madness on our part to be on the streets of Tarnów on such a day. And when we met again that afternoon at the station we were like people who had come out of hell alive, not knowing, not realising how it happened.

The first, bloody deportation from Tarnów took place on 11 June 1942. There were no more deportations to Bełżec that year. In December 1943 there was the last deportation after which Tarnów was proclaimed *'Judenrein '*.

Let Marysia herself tell what she saw and experienced. I found the Birnbaum family at home, after their documents had already been checked. They had the so-called 'good' papers of those in employment. They survived this time – not for long.

MIRIAM

We went to Tarnów together at the beginning of June. Mietek wanted to get news of his father, brothers and friends, and I was planning to go on to Pilzno where my family lived. It was my last effort to convince them that there was no time for hopeless waiting. I had asked them to have their photographs ready for their *Kennkarten*. On my last visit there I had not managed to persuade either my parents or even my sister, who looked Aryan and was a very energetic person – yet she talked about escaping and living on the Aryan side as of something impossible, like a trip to the moon. Her husband's looks did not augur well for his survival. Her two daughters aged seventeen and nine lived a more or less normal life in Pilzno and it seemed that they would be in more danger on the Aryan side. These were illusions against which it was impossible to fight. Even after what I saw in Tarnów, they would not believe that the same fate awaited them.

We arrived in Tarnów on the day of the first, bloody deportation. We said goodbye at the railway station and were to meet there in the afternoon. Before I entered a tram, I was rooted to the spot by a horrendous sight: a column of Jews to be deported, walking or rather dragging along. It was a deportation to death, but these people who were lied to and who lied to each other, were dragging with them bundles, suitcases, parcels – all they were allowed to take with them. And they had their children with them. There was one moment which has stayed in my memory forever: an old woman at the end of this procession was carrying on her back an eiderdown, a red eiderdown tied up with string. The eiderdown kept slipping from her back; she tried to put it back, then gave up and just dragged it behind her, unable to keep up with the others. One of the escorting soldiers kept prodding her with his rifle and shouting something I could not hear. Finally, she dropped the eiderdown, her only worldly possession, which was to protect her from the cold somewhere where they would take her – as she believed – for the rest of her life: not to her death, not to her death. She walked faster, driven by the butt of the rifle, and she joined the rest of the column. I did not yet know what sight awaited me a moment later. I got off the tram at Wałowa Street.

In a side street another column of exiles was forming. Here the SS men were in charge. I could not escape the scene in front of me, I had to watch it. A young man in a long coat had an attack of hysteria – he was crying out loud, sobbing, it was like the whining of a beaten dog. A German flew up to him, a shot was fired, the boy fell on his face, bleeding. The SS man grabbed him by his coat, dragged him along the ground and threw the body to a wall, leaving a trace of blood on the road. I stood petrified, unable to take a step. Suddenly someone took my arm from behind: a man pulled me off and said in a whisper which sounded like a muffled cry, 'Are you crazy? You are not allowed to stop, to look, haven't you seen the posters?'

I had not seen the posters, only later I read that death was the penalty for stopping in the street during the resettlement action, for entering a Jewish flat or taking any Jewish belongings. Disregarding this warning, I went to the house where Mietek's father lived on Panna Maria Street. He was horrified to see me. He said the Germans could be there any moment, they were dragging people out of their homes, I could fall into their hands. He was completely resigned to his fate, he did not attempt to hide, he had not even shaved off his beard. He said he had already lost his wife, Mietek's stepmother, and small daughter, he did not know what had happened to his sons, and he would not try to save himself, he had nothing to live for.

In the same house lived a shoemaker who worked for the Germans. In his workshop he had a shoe with a beautiful shining upper on a last. He showed me this shoe and asked me as if expecting I could give him hope, 'These are shoes for a Gestapo man, so do you think they will leave me alone? After all, I work for the Gestapo, they know it . . . . My wife is in hiding. What do you think?' His hands were shaking, he was caressing the shoe. It was to be his protector, his salvation.

The shoe did not save him. Mietek, when he was next in Tarnów, heard from the people who stayed there after the deportations that the shoemaker was shot in the yard of the house where he lived. His wife who saw what happened from her hiding place, ran out to him and was killed too.

I left, my departure hastened by the fear of these people who pleaded with me to escape because the Germans were already only two houses away. I visited two more flats, inhabited by Jews who had 'good' documents certifying they worked for the Germans. I do not remember their names, but I do remember that I took from one flat – at the request of the family living there – a record player which I gave to some Polish friends of theirs. This mission was so incongruous with the massacre taking place on that day that I just could not understand these people with their request. But I did not want to refuse them, despite the warnings on the German posters.

Mietek and I met at the station as was agreed. We did indeed feel like people who had come out of hell alive. Not only were we unable to talk about what we had seen, but we even found it hard to look each other in the eye. I was relieved to see Mietek board the train for Kraków. He was calm and confident as usual, and I was not worried about him. And he did not try to make me change my plans: he knew I had to go to Pilzno.

My visits home to see my parents, exiled from their farm, always produced complications. After all, I was visiting a small town where probably all the inhabitants – the Jews and the Poles – knew me. I had my Aryan documents with me, but I could only impersonate a Pole until I reached Pilzno. Once there, I would enter the first Jewish home where they would give me an armband with the Star of David and thus armed, I would go to see my family. At that time there wasn't even a ghetto in Pilzno, it was created only three weeks before its final liquidation.

I set off from Tarnów on foot, Pilzno was twenty kilometres away. It was a late June afternoon, I was afraid I would not get there before night. I stood in the road and stopped the first German truck. The soldier sitting next to the driver helped me to climb on some sacks, but I was afraid to go to Pilzno with them. About two kilometres before Pilzno I tapped on their window, and walked the rest of the way. On the hill just outside the town lived the Jewish Rymer family. They supplied me with the armband with the Star of David and I went to my parents' house. I was still horrified by what I had seen in Tarnów and I thought I would find them all equally petrified. To my surprise, I found the atmosphere almost idyllic compared to what was taking place only some twenty kilometres away. The small town was quiet. Yes, people were being taken away to work, some young people had been taken to a camp in Pustkowie near Dębica, but the day-to-day life continued near to normal.

I had an attack of hysteria, I was shouting and crying. They looked at me as if I was crazy. 'What is the matter with you?' said my father. 'What is happening in Tarnów does not concern us at all. There are plenty of Jews there, but here? It is different from Tarnów, nothing will happen to us.'

They did not have any photographs for their Aryan documents ready, and were not prepared for such ventures anyway. It was impossible to convince them. Finally, my father explained his reasons to me: he was eighty-two at the time and he looked like a Polish nobleman. Nobody – long before the war – who did not know him personally, would believe that he was Jewish. He told me he would not be able to pretend he was a Pole and if they did agree to live like this and lie – these were his words 'to lie' – they would not only not save themselves, but would put my life in great danger. My sister thought the same. It was not even that she was resigned to her fate like so many of the others. It was a blind faith against which I was powerless. I felt impotent, distraught, exhausted. It was they who tried to comfort and reassure me. They had enough food, had provisions of flour, potatoes, cereals and cooking fat and tried to use this as an argument to convince me that all would be well. I begged my sister to let at least her older daughter, Litka, come with me. I would take her to Kraków and fix her up somehow. She was seventeen at the time, she had excellent Polish looks, she knew German. I could rely on help from my comrades in the underground. 'I won't part with the children', said my sister. 'Come what may we shall stay together.' At the very last moment, the night before their deportation to Bełżec six weeks later, she sneaked out of the ghetto at night and left her younger daughter, Hania, with her Polish friend, the mother of Ziutka Rysińska. This was the same Ziutka who was an underground courier until the end of the war and her name is mentioned in all the publications about help to the Jews in Kraków during the war. It was she who brought my small niece to Kraków a few days after the deportation at the end of July 1942.

I left Pilzno the following day at dawn, unaware that I had said goodbye to my family forever. As usual, I left wearing the Star of David armband and on the outskirts of the town I threw this dangerous item into a roadside ditch. This time I walked in the opposite direction, to Dębica, eleven kilometres away from Pilzno. I hadn't walked for long when a car stopped with a German in civilian clothes at the wheel. 'Wohin?' he asked briefly – 'Dębica'.

He told me to get in and did not say another word. I was grateful for that, I did not feel like talking. He stopped by the first street in Dębica. I walked to the station and returned to Kraków by train. Mietek was not at home, he was on his way to Lwów.

On the same day, I received from Kłopotowski two *Kennkarten* and addresses of people in Bochnia who were to receive them. I was surprised to find out that one of the *Kennkarten* was destined for the mother of an old friend, Dr Bernard Osiek. When I entered the flat at a given address, I found him and his mother there. I was wearing dark glasses and he did not recognise me at first. I recognised him at once and greeted him in a casual manner, like an acquaintance. I removed my glasses and saw his total amazement. He told me never to take off my glasses if I didn't want to be recognised by someone suspect.

'Everything looks suspect around us,' I said, 'and glasses are not such a foolproof safeguard. All depends on the feel of a situation and experience is the best guide'. I had experience gathered during nearly two years of illegal work, illegal life.

WE BORE WITNESS

Thus I returned to our 'chalk circle', full of dark thoughts, powerless and hurt. I saw people who wanted to save themselves at all cost, who would stake their all upon a single cast of the die, aware that salvation was possible this way and that the only alternative was extermination. Only my nearest and dearest didn't want to accept this truth. I often admired the courage of these people, those Jews whom I supplied with forged documents, and I saw that their looks, demeanour and vocabulary were far from ideal. Today – after years of work in Yad Vashem, after reading hundreds of accounts and listening to dozens of stories told by the survivors – I can better and more fully appreciate their courage. In spite of impossible conditions, they took a decision and saved their lives. It would be hard to determine what percentage of these people survived. I don't think such statistics are possible at all. Only the millions who died can be counted, single graves will never enter the statistics.

Ziutka had only one address in Kraków which enabled her to make contact with us: a clothing factory in the Main Market. The firm belonged, as I already mentioned, to my cousin, Dawid Birnbaum, but at that time in the summer of 1942, his entire family was in Wieliczka and the firm was run by a commissioner. He was the German, Madritsch, who was helping the Jews and saving them in all possible ways. He now has his own tree in Yad Vashem in Jerusalem as one of the 'Just'. At the time another of my cousins, Mituśka Hochberg, still worked in the office at the factory. (She has a mention in various publications as a courier for the Council for Jewish Aid, but she is always mentioned by her first name only, sometimes with an additional unfamiliar second name.) One day Madritsch asked her for a word in private. He advised her to try to obtain Aryan documents for herself and even gave her some money for that purpose. She thus stayed in her post for a time as a Pole, but this was too dangerous. When the factory moved to Podgórze, she stopped working there and I introduced her to the Council for Jewish Aid.

Ziutka's card telling me that she would be coming on such and such a day, bringing the child with her, arrived at the address of the factory. I was to wait for them there. At Ziutka Rysińska's house, the child, snatched from death, was hidden in the attic, in the care of Ziutka's mother, Zofia Skazowa, who was a wonderful woman. After a few days, when things quietened down in the small town, Ziutka arranged for Hania's transfer to Kraków in a German lorry repaired by her stepfather in his workshop. Ziutka and Hania travelled in this lorry by night and they were stopped twice for identity checks. Hania had no documents whatsoever. Ziutka covered her face with a shawl, she was supposedly taking her to a dentist. They arrived in Kraków at dawn when the factory was still closed. When I got there at seven in the morning, I found them sitting on the pavement by the front door, tired and sleepy. God knows how it happened that no German or policeman took an interest in this homeless pair.

This was the beginning of nine-year-old Hania Reich's life as an orphan. She stayed one night in the flat of some friends, the Wcisłos, at Starowiślna Street, then I took Hania to stay temporarily in our flat in Dębniki. But this was not safe, whatever 'safe' meant in our circumstances. At that time we were involved in matters which made us leave our place in Dębniki. Again, Kłopotowski gave us the address of a woman acquaintance at Dietla Street where we stayed for a time without registration. Hania was with us until the time when Jadwiga Kruczkowska, wife of Leon and sister of Wanda Janowska, took her under her roof. Alas, there too Hania was not able to stay longer than a few months. She even went to school while she was there, but finally Jadwiga's son, Adam, got asked once or twice why his cousin resembled a Jewess. Hania did not have particularly Jewish features, she could easily have passed for a Polish child, but she had brown hair and lovely, hazel brown eyes – the eyes of my mother. This was enough to make her look suspicious next to fair-haired Adam. Jadwiga did not even hint that she wanted to get rid of Hania, she just repeated to me what the children were saying. This was enough, I had no right to expose her to danger. Her husband was in a prisoners' camp, she had a hard battle to survive, she had an only son. I couldn't have her safety on my conscience. I then turned to Janka, my friend and confidante from Bronowice, and she, through her contacts and connections with a family of very devout Catholics, found my niece a place in the Albertine Convent in Rząska, not far from Bronowice.

I got to know the life of many Jewish children in convents from post-war stories and accounts read at Yad Vashem, but I also witnessed it myself. It was a safe but sad life. Here too Hania's dark hair and eyes attracted attention. All the other children in the convent had light blond hair, blue eyes. I introduced her there as the daughter of people who for political reasons had been exiled and died in a German camp. I added a further lie that her mother was Ukrainian: I thought that this would explain her different looks.

I don't know if any of the nuns had guessed the truth, nothing was ever mentioned. What confirmed me in my belief that no-one suspected her of being Jewish was that one of the nuns looking after the children said to me several times, 'Do have a word with Hania to take better care of her appearance. Sometimes she looks so untidy, her shoe laces undone, she looks like some Jewess!'

I thought that if there was any suspicion, the nun would not have used such an example.

I went to the convent on Sundays whenever time allowed, to give this child some confidence, some warmth – and I could give her so little. We used to sit in a quiet spot in the beautiful convent garden and I tried to talk with her about our home, our family. I asked her to remember who she was, but not to give herself away. There was really no need for such warnings. She was so secretive, so silent, she never asked about her mother and father. She swallowed her child's tears and I swallowed mine. As many Jewish children to whose lot it had fallen to lead such a life, she went along with the atmosphere of the convent. The children prayed on every occasion, at work and at play. Often, standing behind the door to the hall, I would hear endless litanies and 'Hail Marys'. 'Hail Mary, full of grace . . .', '. . . have mercy upon us . . .'. 'Have mercy upon us . . .' I would think about our great, silent Jewish God. I was never without faith, but turning to God, I thought of my parents who died a martyr's death – and I asked them for salvation for this child.

The hardest experience for me during the Sunday visits was the service in the chapel. I couldn't stay outside so I sat in the back. I knelt with the others and watched as the children entered in a line, Hania first because she was the tallest, and it was she who would repeat three times, 'Blessed be the Most Holy Sacrament, now and for ever and ever. Amen.'

One day the priest who taught the children religion at the Convent asked to see me and told me that Hania was the best of his flock. Her diligence and intelligence were outstanding, it was obvious that she came from a good and devout family.

I thought thankfully that she did not have, like so many other Jewish children, to stay in hiding for months and years in a cubby-hole, behind a wardrobe, in a bunker – wasn't this wonderful? What I felt in my heart was not important, did not count in those days. I was grateful that fate allowed this child to breathe in air, to be out in the sun – and to survive.

I might perhaps write about how things turned out after the war in the second, postwar part of our memoirs. Three years of work after the war in the department of Children's Care in the Jewish Committee in Kraków gave me a lot of experience of children who had been saved from the Holocaust, but were often left deeply hurt and psychologically damaged.

4

SOME OF OUR CLIENTS

MORDECAI

The experience gained during the years of occupation at the cost of risking one's life every day and every hour has taught me to view Polish anti-semitism objectively. It was not easy to find it in one's heart to be objective at a time when carriages full of Jews condemned to a cruel death in extermination camps stood on railway lines, and in a train almost next to them in a carriage where I sat among Poles as one of them, a discussion was going on about all sorts of 'crimes', supposedly committed by the Jews: they were work-shy, they cheated their customers, they saved a few grams of sugar on each kilogram they sold and got rich that way, they were exploiters and liars, etc., etc. And now they were reaping their just rewards – the wrath of God had fallen on them in Hitler's guise.

I listened to these conversations and thought about Kłopotowski, about all the Poles with whom we worked and who put their own lives in danger, and who did everything they could to help, to save at least one life, the life of one Jew, one child. Was it possible that these people belonged to the same nation, that they grew in the same land, bloodstained with the death of hundreds of thousands of innocent victims?

Among the passengers in one carriage loudly demonstrating their joy, there were some who remained silent. I knew that like myself they condemned this blind hatred and endless stupidity, but that they could not, dared not, open their mouths. It was only possible to express satisfaction in public with the fate of the Jews, it was dangerous to condemn it.

Let me digress here. After the war, we talked to Mrs Tonia

Seiden who was given shelter with her small boy by some farmer. She was in the barn with her child and heard this same farmer talking to his neighbours about the Jews, 'If I met a Jew here', he declared loudly, 'I would kill him with my axe.' This gave him credibility and allayed any suspicion.

No amount of examples out of my own experience will ever exhaust the subject of the Poles and the Jews under the German occupation. This score will remain unsettled forever and the only answer to all sorts of questions and discussions will be the courage to speak the truth. We and the Poles owe it to history to speak the truth no matter how unpleasant.

At this time, after the first expulsion of the Tarnów Jews, I had an acquaintance who was in hiding in Mościce near Tarnów with the 'T.' family. Janka T., a teacher, my acquaintance's girlfriend and future wife, hid him in the attic of her family home. His name was Józek Birken. It got him a *Kennkart* via Kłopotowski in the name of Józef Kowalik and I visited him quite often. He was very anxious for me to come because he thought these visits greatly cheered up Mrs T., Janka's mother, who could not accept, morally, that 'this Jew' was hiding in her house. Józek had asked me to try to visit him at the beginning of the week, because every Sunday Mrs T. would return from church with renewed hatred towards the Jews. Mrs T. talked to me openly about it, even though she knew I was Jewish.

I don't know what kind of subjects were chosen by the vicar in her church, but after every Sunday sermon Mrs T., a devout Catholic, would say, looking me straight in the eye, 'Jesus will never forgive me for giving shelter to this Jew under my roof. I cannot live this life of sin any longer!'

'Who are you talking to, Mrs T., you know that I am a Jew too.'

She would reply with a typical lack of logic that I was a 'different Jew' because I was blond, I had blue eyes and a fair complexion. As I was lucky enough not to need her attic, she must have thought being friendly with me was not a sin. Anyway, I used to manage to persuade her a little that Jesus would not punish her for saving somebody's life, and after each conversation she would be calmer – until the next Sunday.

Mrs T.'s son, a ex-officer in the Polish Army, could not understand how I could travel by train and not be afraid. He himself, he said, was terrified when he had to go to Kraków once in six months, and I was totally unconcerned. I had no intention of telling him under what pressure I undertook each journey, how much willpower and apparent coolness I had to muster. I used to turn it into a joke. 'I've got eyes in the back of my head', I would say. 'I can see danger without looking and I know how to avoid it.'

In this joke, like in any other, there was a grain of truth. My instinct was so well developed that it led me and I allowed myself to be led by it. In my intricate, dangerous life I could not always listen to the voice of reason and often I had suddenly to abandon a plan I had worked out. Sometimes miracles happened – there is no other word for it – there were moments when one came safe and well out of situations which could have ended tragically. I experienced this in connection with Józek Birken. He asked me to supply him with cartridges for his gun, which he kept hidden in the attic. This was much later, when I was working with another Pole, Władek Wójcik, who was later to become secretary of the Council for Jewish Aid. It was he who supplied me with the cartridges. I simply put them in the pocket of my raincoat, thinking that it would be easy to get rid of them in case of a search. But the search came so unexpectedly during a train journey that there was no question of emptying my pocket quickly. The train was packed. I was standing in the corridor when suddenly two SS men started feeling the pockets of all the passengers. Luckily, they did not give the order usual in such cases: 'Hände hoch!'. They were in a great hurry. When they came to me, I pushed back the sides of my raincoat. My jacket and trouser pockets were empty. One of the SS men felt them with one quick movement and they went away. I cannot explain how I felt. I was alive – that was all.

MIRIAM

Of the many and various candidates wishing to assume an Aryan identity, I recall a few, the most characteristic ones. The others fell into oblivion, there is no sign of them in our private archives from the times of occupation, containing many documents from the time of our work in the Council for Jewish Aid.

To one of our meetings Zygmunt brought a young Jewish boy and said to me, 'He will tell you himself what this is about. Get his photo and all the details and leave them for me in the shop. Arrange a meeting with him in two days.' The 'shop' was our meeting place at Karmelicka Street which I have already mentioned.

The meeting took place on the banks of the Vistula River. The Jewish boy had 'good' Polish looks, he was composed and he spoke perfect Polish. All these were trump cards but, best of all, he had a very original idea. He had a friend, a Pole about the same age as him, who agreed to have a duplicate made of his own genuine *Kennkart*, on the condition that the new 'Aryan' would leave Kraków immediately and go as far away as possible.

The boy gave me all the details from the real *Kennkart* plus his photo, and said, 'I do hope you can do it. I shall be waiting here the day after tomorrow.'

'Where will you go?' I asked.

'To the East. I shall cross the border into Romania. I know this is possible, I have some contacts . . .'

A lot could happen in two days. I went to meet him, with the new *Kennkart*, with my heart pounding. Nothing had happened, the boy was waiting for me. When there was nobody around, he took his fingerprints and signed the *Kennkart* with his new name. Mietek and I always carried the box with the ink needed for the fingerprints. We did the officials at 'Der Stadthauptmann der Stadt Krakau' proud!

As we were saying goodbye, the boy said, 'If I am stopped and checks are made at the police station in Kraków, they will find that all is in order, because the police have got the copy of the real *Kennkart*.'

I agreed with him, he was right that they had a duplicate of the *Kennkart* at the police station. The main problem was that they should not start their investigations with the one which was most dangerous to a man. But we did not mention this.

'We have to believe that all will be well, you look so Polish.'

I tried to speak with deep conviction, experience had taught me that the help we were giving to all those endangered people was not just about supplying them with documents. I do not know and I shall probably never know whether he was lucky. I did not know his real name.

The strict rules of the underground work said the fewer Jews' and underground workers' names we knew the safer, in case of an investigation. Sometimes we encountered tragicomical situations in our work. Zygmunt never told my Jewish clients that I myself was Jewish. They did not consider me therefore as a co-sufferer in their tragedy and in spite of their undoubtedly warm feelings towards a Pole such as me, I often sensed a lack of communication in the most personal matters. In their eyes I belonged to a people – persecuted by the Germans indeed – but in an infinitely better situation compared to their Jewish tragedy. We often dealt with people who had already lost those nearest to them – their children, most painful of all, often their parents and brothers and sisters. Even when they shared their unhappiness with me, they did not do so readily, and I felt that they were not all that convinced of my deep sympathy for them. After I had lost my own family, I had moments of weakness which made me, quite unnecessarily, reveal my true identity. It seemed to me that it would make it easier for them to bear their own fate, knowing that I shared their unhappiness. These were vain hopes. Zygmunt would get very cross with me on learning about my indiscretion. Most of the time I had to accept his instructions in silence, but it caused me great unhappiness.

One day, Zygmunt brought me a *Kennkart* in the name of Helena Zając, completely ready except for fingerprints and the signature which I was to see to, but this time I also had another task. Zygmunt found a Polish family who agreed to take in a Jewish woman as a servant, but on certain conditions: the woman had to believe that her employers did not know that she was Jewish; that they had been told that she had to find a safer place for political reasons, and needed to be somewhere where she was not known to anybody. Political reasons could mean anything: in this case it was said that her husband and son had been arrested and she would have been too if she had not escaped in time. As she was to appear as a Pole, she had to be prepared for this new role, mainly she had to be coached in Catholic religion. Ironically, this task was assigned by Zygmunt to me. Just in case, he asked me, 'Will you manage this? Do you know enough about it?'

I did and it was not because I had studied the Catholic religion for my own use as did many Jews when assuming their Aryan identity. I had learned about the customs of the Catholic religion in my family home where there were always some Polish workers, and life in the country was not lived in isolation. For instance, apart from four families of farm hands living in a separate building, there were two girls who lived in the house as part of the family. In addition, there were two unmarried labourers who ate their meals in our kitchen. They all celebrated their holidays in our house and we, as children, were always interested in their customs. Not to mention that every Zosia and Kasia tried, in their simplicity, to teach us something about the Catholic faith, maybe in the vain hope that they could make us into real Catholics. To us as children the most fascinating thing was Christmas. A Christmas tree would be put in the servants' hall and we took part enthusiastically in adorning its green branches, smelling of resin, with sweets, nuts, apples, paper angels and multicoloured candles which were the same as the ones lit on the Hanukah holiday. Nobody prevented us from sitting down to Christmas Eve dinner with the servants. I have kept in my memory all the traditional Christmas Eve dishes and I could, if any occupation situation demanded it, help in preparing them. On the Catholic holiday of Easter, we watched how food was prepared in a basket and taken to church to be blessed, how a blessed egg was shared on Resurrection Day, etc., etc. How was I to know that years later all these accessories of an alien religion would prove useful in our double life?

This time I was to teach Mrs Helena Zając how to behave during holidays so as not to reveal her true origins. But it turned out that this candidate for a devout Pole was a hard nut to crack. Zygmunt gave me, together with her *Kennkart*, a prayer book, somewhat worn out to preserve the appearances. She was to sign it with her name and smudge the signature a little so that it would not look too new. When I tried to tell her how and where to look for the relevant prayers, she answered me rather scornfully, 'I shall find them all right, I can read'.

She was greatly infuriated by her new name: Zając, Helena Zając. This did not surprise me. I have often come across this fact, that most Jews on Aryan papers preferred to have names ending with 'ski'. I could not blame them (after all, I was 'Górska' and Mietek was 'Piotrowski'). Helena simply took it literally, 'Do I look like a hare (zając)?' she asked me bitterly.

I explained that this was not my fault, that I received the prepared documents from Zygmunt. This made her even more cross.

'He knows me,' she said, 'how could he give me such a name!'

SOME OF OUR CLIENTS

I assured her that such a name sounded less suspicious because it was a common name. She had no choice but to accept it, but our worst showdown came just before Easter when I was trying to teach her the holiday customs. I told her to remember that Good Friday was a day of fast and of visits to church, that on Saturday the food was taken to church to be blessed and on Easter Day there was a special service in church and then everybody returned home for an equally special and big meal during which a 'blessed egg' was shared. The eggs were usually painted beforehand with special paints and they were called 'pisanki', etc. Mrs Zając listened to my lecture rather indulgently and then asked me a question which frightened me. 'I know all this, just tell me about breaking the wafer with others . . .'

'We are in a fine mess', I thought and said very sternly, 'Heaven forbid that you should get your religious holidays mixed up. A wafer is broken on Christmas Eve, not at Easter. Such a mistake may have dire results'.

Helena was surprised and embarrassed but she obviously decided to score a point and said haughtily, 'All you have told me is not that important. If I started teaching you about *our* celebrations of Passover, you would never learn it!'

I had to swallow humbly this riposte and try to smooth things over. There was one important matter on which I could not offer Mrs Zając any guidance, though I suspected that this would be another examination for her to pass: confession and Holy Communion. These were serious matters in the Catholic religion and I never attempted to give instructions on this to any of the Jewish 'Aryans'. Happily, neither I nor Mietek was forced into this kind of dissimulation. I did not go to church for the sake of appearances because nobody checked up on me, nor did I wear a cross on my neck though I recommended this camouflage device to others. I did sometimes visit churches where I had rendezvous with other couriers. We sometimes left the underground mail on previously agreed church benches to be collected by other couriers. To tell the truth, these were sometimes breathing spells – it was bliss to sit down in a dark church for fifteen minutes of peace and silence, and perhaps illusory, but none the less longed for, safety.

Once, in May 1942, Zygmunt sent me with some message to a village near Kraków whose name I do not recall. I was to take to a family of Polish socialists, members of the Polish Socialist Party, an underground publication and written instructions. It was evening and these people were getting ready for the May Service. They suggested that I should go along with them. I could not get out of it and I took part in the service. And there would have been nothing unusual about it if it had not been for something that happened much later. One day, soon after the war, I met by chance in the street a girl who used to be a cook at my relatives' before the war. She was very glad to see me and she told me that she had seen me at a May Service in this village. 'I did not come up to you', she said, 'because I thought maybe it was not a good thing that we knew each other and that I knew, I knew everything . . .'

There was no telling who would take an interest in us and when – not always, as in this case, with good intentions. This girl was friendly, and above all, wise. It could have been otherwise.

The order about the confiscation of fur coats and skis from Jews was announced and carried out in Kraków in December 1941. The harsh winter in Poland in 1941–2, which was even harsher on the Soviet territories, came as a surprise to the German Army which had been promised by Hitler a 'Blitzkrieg' similar to that in Poland. The German soldiers therefore needed to be kitted out with Jewish furs and skis.

My skis were at home in the country at the time. On my first visit there I broke and burned them, not without melancholy – these two wooden boards and sticks reminded me of so many happy times. I took my ski boots with me and I left my modest fur collar on my winter coat as one more proof of my being Aryan. As I later found out, the two fur-lined coats belonging to my sister and brother-in-law were given for storage to our neighbours in the country. (Even these fur coats have got their place in my war biography!)

I mention the trivial fur collar on my coat because it is connected with another, more important, event. Among the *Kennkarten* supplied to me by Kłopotowski, I found one day in winter 1942, one which greatly moved me: I saw a familiar face on the photograph – this was no other than Mietek Steinbach, an ear, nose and throat specialist and Dr Schwarzbard's assistant at the Jewish Hospital in Kraków – a constant com-

SOME OF OUR CLIENTS

panion at our pre-war sessions in the 'Krysztal' and 'Bizanc' cafés. We used to gather there to read the papers and Cyrankiewicz used to joke that we made our living by paying thirty groszes for a small black coffee and reading papers to the value of two złotys. I knew that the Schwarzbards had left Kraków and gone to the East at the beginning of the war, but I knew nothing about Steinbach. Now, I was told to take a *Kennkart* to him to the hospital in the Kielce ghetto.

The hospital stood at the border of the ghetto and the entrance was from the Aryan side. It was January 1943: I appeared before Mietek Steinbach in my fur-collar coat and in a fur hat. Mietek was brought at my request to the hospital waiting room. It is difficult for me today to describe this meeting, which came as a complete surprise to him. But in his agitation and possibly fear at the sight of me, he noticed first of all my fur accessories.

Not realising that I was there as a Pole, he dragged me to the nearest hospital infirmary and simply wrung his hands. 'Fur? Marysia, don't you realise?'

'Shut up', I said quickly, 'I am here as a Pole, do you understand?' Only then did we greet each other warmly and possibly with tears in our eyes, but this I do not remember exactly.

Dr Steinbach was rather optimistic. There were about a dozen Jewish doctors in the ghetto, he was the personal physician of some important SS man, on whom he operated for an abscess in the throat. The operation was a success which accounted for Dr Steinbach's optimism. He wanted to have a *Kennkart* just in case and this was why he arranged to have a contact in Kraków and had reached Kłopotowski and me in such a strange, roundabout way. He was so happy at our unexpected meeting that he would not agree to my immediate return to Kraków. But this was not the only reason: he brought with him two aspiring Aryans – they both worked in a clothing factory without any previous training. They gave me their photographs and personal details. I arranged with them that I would return in a week with the *Kennkarten* and we arranged exactly where we would meet. Just in case, we were to meet not at the hospital, but by the barbed wires where there was a hidden entrance to the ghetto.

Steinbach was in touch with his close friend, Zygmunt

Gross, and I think – I do not remember exactly – that they made contact through Gross's wife. After my return to Kraków, I found that I had to go to Warsaw to meet Gross – who was in hiding with some Polish family in Żoliborz, and to talk to him about preparations for Steinbach's escape. I found Gross at the address I was given – a quiet, self-possessed, elegant man. He was ready to put up Steinbach in his room for a time, before he could find something better, and the whole thing looked – for those days – very simple and hopeful.

A week later I was in Kielce again, the meeting with the two aspiring Aryans took place in the clothing factory in a fitting cubicle. Naturally, clothes were made there for Germans only. My clients put their fingerprints on their *Kennkarten*, they signed themselves with their new names and – I do not know what happened to them.

But Steinbach, who this time came with me to the meeting in the factory, had not yet decided to leave the ghetto. I realised only later that he lacked the courage to do it, and I often reproached myself for not having offered to accompany him on his journey to Warsaw. I reported to him on my meeting with Gross and on Gross's willingness to take him in and help him to set himself up in Warsaw. For me, this was such a decisive argument that it had not occurred to me for a moment that he would not accept this plan. But he waited and deluded himself that his German protector would take care of him. And so he waited until March 1943, when in one of a series of 'operations' in the Kielce ghetto, fourteen Jewish doctors and their families were shot dead at the Jewish cemetery. Dr Mieczysław Steinbach was one of them.

Nothing was as painful as the knowledge that all the efforts made to save a life were in vain, particularly in this case when Zygmunt Gross's willingness to receive the fugitive gave him an exceptional chance of survival.

I was used to travelling by train, I never had any mishaps, but this time something happened which simply frightened me. And it all started by stupid chance. After leaving the Kielce ghetto I was not feeling well. I was depressed after my meeting with Steinbach and those two others. I could see that Steinbach was not ready to leave the ghetto and the two others had no definite plans. We all knew that a *Kennkart* and even the best documents alone were not enough. What was also needed were

SOME OF OUR CLIENTS

contacts, courage and determination. I had nothing to offer these people; help for the Jews was not yet organised at that time. The organisation 'Żegota' had not yet been born, and only someone with personal contacts and opportunities could survive using the forged documents. Steinbach was the only one of the three who had such opportunities but even this had failed.

I felt hungry and I entered a restaurant. I feel sick until this day at the thought of the meal I had there. I recall so well the rancid fat in which my cutlet was fried. I felt sick the moment I left the restaurant and I had to stop several times to be sick on my way to the railway station. I also had a terrible migraine and when I went to the ladies at the station for a quick wash, I looked in the mirror and had a shock: the face I saw was the face of a Jewess. I could not recognise myself. I bought a ticket to Kraków, but when I came on the platform and saw the crowd of people waiting for this train, I knew for sure that having to fight for a seat or even for just getting on the train, in my present state, would be the end of me. Anybody looking at me would have no doubt that I had escaped from the ghetto.

When the train arrived at the station, I took an instant decision. I saw two carriages 'Nur für Deutsche' nearly empty as usual. Without a moment's hesitation I entered the first compartment. I closed the door and lay on a bench. I felt immediate relief. I was in such a state that I had no other fear than the fear of recurring nausea. Lying down, plus the silence of this place – as opposed to what was taking place outside – somehow had a calming effect on me and all that was left was enormous fatigue and a headache. When the train started and nobody bothered me for the moment, the monotonous clatter of the wheels put me to sleep as easily as if I were in my own bed, far from the war. I must have been asleep for an hour or longer before I was woken up by the door being pushed open. I did not want to open my eyes, but I had no choice, someone had lightly touched my arm. I sat up, still half-asleep, and saw two German gendarmes standing in front of me. Their friendly smiles disappeared when, obeying their order, I showed them my *Kennkart*. 'You are Polish', said one of them. 'Can't you read? This is a compartment for the Germans.'

The fact that I was a Pole in the eyes of this German brought back my powers of logical thinking. In my very Polish, thick

German, searching for words, and at the same time smiling with innocent coqueterie, I explained that I had such a terrible headache, and there was such a crowd there, and here I was in nobody's way . . . etc. The greenish pallor of my face must have convinced them, because one of the Germans motioned me to stay and said, 'Na, da schlafen sie weiter.'

They left without waiting for my grateful 'Danke schön', closing the door behind them. I thought that they must have been the better kind of Germans because it could have all ended differently: they could have thrown me out of this wagon at the nearest station and pointed me towards some shady characters who were always present on trains. As to my German, I never pretended when I had to communicate with the Germans that I could not understand or speak their language. I have discovered that this irritated them terribly. But, as I said, my German was so devoid of any trace of a German accent that they never bothered to ask where I learned it. Suspicion could be aroused either by an excellent German pronunciation or a mixture of Yiddish and German. But even this was not a hard and fast rule. Anyway, in my case, neither my German nor my Polish was a handicap.

'Travel broadens the mind' – this proverb was everyday reality for us, if not in the sense in which it was intended. We did not learn about other countries, landscapes, culture or art, but we learned to react quickly and almost faultlessly in dangerous situations. We both travelled a lot and therefore did not lack occasion to broaden our minds. Mietek did it with unnecessary bravado sometimes, with an optimistic faith in his lucky stars. For me it was not so simple, I was not an optimist in those times. I don't even know if it was courage. It is hard to define it. One day, when I volunteered for some special task, 'Teodor' said to me, 'It is not that you are so brave, but you have no sense of reality.'

He was probably right, but not a hundred per cent, because in every situation I had to remember that I was Jewish. Even when we were involved in purely Polish matters of underground work, not connected with aid to the Jews, we were always doubly at risk. It sometimes happened that in a train or even in a tram some man would look at me with more than casual interest. This would immediately put me on my guard, even though it could simply be a man eyeing a woman stranger.

SOME OF OUR CLIENTS

But I was vigilant and not as divorced from reality as claimed by 'Teodor'. But he was right in one thing, because even in the most dangerous moments I was unable to imagine that I could find myself in the hands of the Gestapo. Was this good or bad? No one can answer such a theoretical question. Even the fact that I have survived is no answer to it.

Ziutka Rysińska had become our nearly constant companion since she brought my small niece and then my brother-in-law to Kraków. She was a brave courier and full of initiative. From one of her journeys to our home town, Pilzno, she brought the remains of my family's possessions. There was not much left: my mother's gold, old-fashioned watch on a long chain, my sister's and her husband's watches, and my sister's wedding ring and engagement ring with a small, very modest, diamond. I kept the two rings and we sold the rest. Each of these items was of great sentimental value to me, but our finances were in a perilous state.

I learned from my brother-in-law that the two fur-lined winter coats belonging to him and his wife had not been handed over to the Germans, but were stored by a Polish family, our neighbours over many years. In the winter of 1942, when we simply had no means to pay for my brother-in-law's stay and were concerned about little Hania, who had to have winter clothes, and money was needed at least for her keep, I decided to make the journey to go and recover these two coats. I could not ask Ziutka to go, even though she was prepared to do it. She was a familiar face there and her contacts with us could not be revealed.

It was a cold, white winter. I got off the train at the small station in the village of Czarna between Tarnów and Dębica. It was the same station from which I used to travel to Kraków before the war. Many people there knew me, including the Polish railwaymen who lived locally. They used to come and buy grass from our meadows as fodder for their cattle. But it wasn't difficult to get off the train quickly and continue on my way. I knew every path and did not have to ask the way. I did not try to arrange for a cart to get to my destination. I decided to walk through the woods which stretched in a continuous wide strip between Tarnów and Dębica. The distance by road was eleven kilometres, whereas the way through the woods was shorter, but very arduous. The paths which were trodden out in summer, were now covered with snow. I walked, guided by instinct: after all I was born and bred in the country. As it turned out, I was right. Just before the early winter dusk, I came out of the forest onto the snow-covered meadows outside the village of Wygoda. The first cottage, one kilometre away, was the home of the Niedziela family whom I knew well. Three women lived there: a widow and her two daughters, Wikcia and Zosia who was already married. These two girls, a few years older than me, had been my constant childhood companions. They used to work on our estate. They were charming, intelligent girls, eager to learn and to make friends. I used to lend them my books and we read Polish poetry together. In these uncertain times I trusted them, but even so decided to remain in the forest until dark.

I stood on the outskirts of the forest, leaning on the trunk of a pine tree and looked dry-eyed at the landscape of my youth which had begun and ended here. In the distance I could see the red roof of our house on the hill. On these meadows, now covered with snow, were maybe still imprinted the footsteps of my father who walked here hundreds of times. Maybe the prints of our bare feet were still here, left when we walked in damp grass in the spring, gathering wild flowers. Those were not yet memories. They are memories today. Then, a few months after the 'resettlement' of my family – as the road to death in Bełzec is now called – it was raw despair which made the heart contract like a clenched fist. Why had I come here, for Heaven's sake? For the fur coats? They were all that was left of my parents' possessions after thirty years of work on this land, which was to them home, life and hope for a peaceful old age. Over the roof of my childhood home, over the roofs of peasant cabins, trails of smoke rose in the clear early evening air. The living were cooking supper. Time to go.

It was dusk when I reached the cabin of my friends. I did not weep even when they sobbed at the sight of me and embraced me, cold and numb. I drank a mug of hot milk and told them why I had come. I do not want to go into details. They sent Zosia's husband for the farmer who had the coats in store. He brought me one at night so that the neighbours would not see him. He was right in saying I should not take the two together. But we had an exchange which gave me a taste of the bitterness of what was called the reclamation of Jewish possessions. I asked him to give me a lift to the station the next day, as it would be hard to walk through the forests again, but he refused. He was afraid and he had every right to be. I was a person whose very existence was a danger to others.

I slept the night under an enormous, warm eiderdown. I was given some wonderful brown bread with butter to take with me, bread of which each bite tasted of my lost childhood. I walked to the station by the same way through the woods. This time it was not the walking that was hard. The most difficult thing was standing in a short queue to get my ticket to Kraków and waiting for the train. I had not timed my arrival at the station precisely and I had to wait for forty-five minutes in the cold waiting room where each pair of eyes could bring disaster. Here neither my Aryan looks nor my *Kennkart* would save me. Nobody greeted me, no one approached me. Behind my back I could hear whispers exchanged by the people in the queue. A few of them knew me, but there was not one enemy among them. I believe until this day that I was watched over by my father and the memory he had left among those people.

I did not give up on the second coat. I repeated this journey without any incident. It gave us some cash for our most immediate needs.

5

FUGITIVES FROM THE JANOWSKI CAMP

MORDECAI

Back in 1942 – I don't remember the exact date – Adam Rysiewicz gave me the following task to carry out: to find, when I went to Lwów, a certain Max Boruchowicz, who was known to have been in Lwów during the Soviet occupation. This was the very first time that a complete stranger was involved. Up till now only personal friends, colleagues, and acquaintances had been involved, whom I knew through 'Teodor' or Kłopotowski, at least by sight.

I began investigating Boruchowicz during a chance meeting with Natek Schönberg from Tarnów. I caught sight of him in Lwów wearing a Jewish policeman's cap. He was somewhat taken aback when he saw me; how could it be otherwise? It could well be that he was a bit wary of any contacts with an 'Aryan' like me, but he did follow me into a gate entrance, as he was curious to hear news from Tarnów and common acquaintances. I didn't want to prolong our conversation, as in his position it might have become dangerous for him to have anything to do with a Pole. I came straight to the point: did he ever come across the surname Boruchowicz and did he know anything about the man? No, he did not know this name, but promised to ask around in the *Judenrat* where his brother worked. We made a date to meet in the same place the next day. What he told me was not very hopeful. The information he did have was that Boruchowicz had been amongst a group of Jews who had been hanged. The only thing he was not sure about was whether this had been Max or someone else. I returned to Kraków with this information, which I passed on to 'Teodor'.

FUGITIVES FROM THE JANOWSKI CAMP

The whole story might well have ended here. 'Teodor' dropped the whole thing but for me the business was not closed. For the following few months, during every one of my visits, I made discreet attempts to question every Janowski Camp inmate who came to work in our factory, Niesel und Kämmer, about Boruchowicz. I got a negative answer every time, they didn't know him or anything about him. Miriam, who had known Boruchowicz before the war, had by now given up asking me if I had found anything or not. I could not forget about it, no matter how I tried. It was strange, as the man involved was neither kith nor kin to me. I knew nearly all the camp prisoners by sight, so I was able to spot any newcomers and I asked every one of them about Boruchowicz. It turned into a kind of obsession for me. I didn't discuss it with anyone else in Kraków, but deep inside me there existed a kind of subconscious conviction that I must not give up on this.

In September 1943, shortly before the camp was finally liquidated, I noticed another new face among the prisoners. According to Grubner, he was replacing someone who was ill. I asked him if he would make it possible for me to have a quick word with him. He appeared in the office during the lunch break. (One should mention the fact that during this period, the period of great German setbacks on the eastern front, one would rarely see any of the factory directors in the office, as they had their own problems to deal with, like shipping stolen property to their great Reich.) Again, the same question about Boruchowicz, and this time a quite unexpected positive reply: yes, he did know him and they lived in the same barracks.

I again asked Grubner, the person responsible for the group of workers, to substitute Boruchowicz for another prisoner in this group. But Grubner had reservations, which were entirely without foundation, namely, would this Boruchowicz trust the whole undertaking, would he not suspect a trap? I knew just what to do about that eventuality. When we had discussed the possibility of my meeting Boruchowicz, in Kraków, we had taken this possibility into account. Then I had an idea, and I asked Miriam for a small photograph of herself skiing, taken in 1938 in Zakopane. I hoped that Boruchowicz would recognise a familiar face and would realise that he had nothing to fear. At this stage this small, faded photograph made its way to the camp. The very next day Boruchowicz appeared in the factory in place of another prisoner. Our conversation was brief and to the point. At this stage, he had established his 'connections' in the camp, and in answer to my question whether he would be able to organise an ID card photograph of himself he gave a positive answer. 'Keep a look-out,' I said. 'I will come back in four days' time to get the pictures. Is it possible for one of your comrades to ring the office to tell me where I can pick them up? ' Such a possibility did exist.[1]

That was all for the present. But Boruchowicz was very keen to know who it was who was trying to save him and which party was involved. The Socialist Party? The Zionists? I had no intention of telling him all about my activities during those few months. 'I am saving you,' I said curtly. 'Is that not enough for you?' It was enough.

I was excited by this encounter and I think that Boruchowicz felt the same. Ahead of him was the difficult road out of the extermination camp, but in the past others had managed to escape and I believed that he would manage it too. My project was not finished, but the very thought that, after all, my perseverance did not go to waste and that, at last, I was returning to Kraków with some good news, increased my store of strength and energy, as tends to happen in similar circumstances. During this period, the Żegota Jewish Aid Council was already established in the Kraków area. The few Jews remaining were in the camps and sooner or later they would be liquidated. In addition to these few, a tiny handful – and when compared to those already murdered it was only a handful – lived in hiding or, like us, were using 'Aryan' papers. It was not only for its material aid that the organisation was important for

[1] Jehuda Eizman, an engineer, had been a prisoner in the Janowski Camp, where he used the surname Landenheim. He now lives in Tel-Aviv. He gives the following account of the details relating to the telephone contacts with the camp which made it easier for Boruchowicz to escape and for several other prisoners after him as well. In 1943 Wilhaus, the Janowski Camp commander, had given him an office job working for the Viennese firm Territ which was supplying building materials to the camp. The offices were on Jagiellońska Street and the prisoner had free use of the German firm Niesel und Kämmer through whose facilities contact was established and in the same way the contact between Mieczyslaw, Piotrowski and Borwicz was kept up. (Eizman says that throughout this period he was convinced that Mr Piotrowski was a Pole.) Contacts with Żegota in Kraków eventually led to a meeting with the contact Ziutka Rysińska, until Eizman got his own identity card and escaped. In Kraków he was taken care of by members of Żegota who arranged for him to cross the Slovak border and finally to reach Budapest.

this handful. No less important was the consciousness that someone was still thinking and caring about them in this criminal, evil world.

In Kraków, the secretary of Żegota was Władek Wójcik, and he was also the first person to whom I passed news of Boruchowicz. Four days later, as was agreed, I again went to Lwów to fetch the photos.

I went! How simple this sounds to someone who has no idea what was going on at that time in the Kraków railway station. And most probably in all the others as well. As usual I chose the night train in order to be able to take the phone call from Janowski Camp. I always used to arrive just before departure time to avoid having to walk up and down the platform. The place was usually swarming with informers.

On this occasion there was panic and consternation. At this stage the Germans were moving their Army and ammunition eastwards on such a scale that frequently there was no room for Poles even in the passenger train, unless they happened to have a swastika in their lapel. I had no swastika, however I did have my own dangerous insignia. But I knew I had to get on that train and had to be in the factory at nine o'clock the next morning to pick up the photographs and return to Kraków with them. A man's life depended on whether or not I could work this miracle. The threat of destruction hung over the Janowski Camp, soon it might have been too late. The German police were in full action, hitting people over the head with truncheons and throwing Poles out of the waiting room. In this state of commotion there was no time for checking of documents, the truncheon or rifle butt was a good enough argument. I pushed my way through the crowd and went straight for the ticket window. My expression was apparently so self-assured that no-one tried to stop me.

I asked for a ticket to Lwów, speaking German just in case. A ticket collector was standing at the entrance to the platform with two Germans in civilian clothes next to him. 'Sind Sie Deutsche? ' asked one of them.

'Volksdeutsch', I replied without hesitation.

I did not stop to think about the possible consequences of telling such a lie. If I had not managed to carry it off, my fate would have been sealed and my contact with Boruchowicz would have been broken off at this most vital stage. All three of them looked at me and I managed to hold their gaze. They did not demand any documents. It was only afterwards when I was sitting in the train, it occurred to me what did happen and what might have happened during those few seconds: a few seconds between life and death. There was not a single Pole on this train besides me.

When I arrived in Lwów, I witnessed yet another event. Here the Gestapo were using dogs. The Poles were milling round in a great crowd, attempting to get on to an overcrowded train on the verge of departure. One of the Gestapo men set his wolf dog on them. With a terrifying growl, the dog attacked the defenceless crowd. He had been trained not to bite, just to tear at the clothing. Suddenly a shot was heard. It was an Italian officer, who had apparently found himself at the station by accident, who shot the SS man's dog. Petrified with fear I watched what would happen now. The SS man drew his gun with a violent movement, but after a short exchange of words put it back in his pocket. This extraordinary incident set the seal on the last twelve hours.

In Lwów everything went according to plan. I arrived in the office at nine a.m. and awaited news. I was sitting in Director Köller's office and it was he who took the call from Grubner and handed me the receiver. After a short conversation I said that Grubner would like me to go to the factory. The factory was several kilometres away from the main office. The Director politely suggested that I should go along with Holub in the factory car. I picked up the photos from Boruchowicz and we discussed the next meeting. During the few days I spent in Kraków, I handed the photographs over to our outpost dealing with documents and I confirmed where and when the contacts would be waiting for the fugitive in order to take him to Kraków and then I proceeded to Lwów with these directions to give Boruchowicz the final instructions. All this sounds so straightforward and simple, as if it concerned some innocent excursions on the Kraków–Lwów line. But it was not at all easy, neither for me, nor for the camp fugitive, where the whole company could pay with its life for the escape of one single Jew.

But it did succeed. One September day, I do not recollect the exact date, Ziutka Rysińska and Tadeusz Bilewicz went to Lwów with an identity card in the name of Michał Borucki and a train assistant's document. They picked up the fugitive in a prearranged place on Słoneczna Street, left Lwów by the night train and arrived in Kraków in the morning. Władek Wójcik and I were waiting at the station: he was supposed to find a hiding place for Boruchowicz.

The three of us set off, then Władek falls behind somewhat and I try to encourage yesterday's prisoner taking his first steps as a free man. But this freedom is only a semblance of freedom. I am telling him to stride boldly, not to look behind him and not to look down when passing the group of policemen which just happen to be coming from the opposite direction.

'It's easy for you to talk,' says Boruchowicz.

I understand that he is referring to me, the Pole Piotrowski. So, in order to give him courage I show my hand.

'I am what you are,' not using the dangerous word 'Jew'.

This was a complete surprise to him, for he was aware of the fact that every time I had come to Lwów in connection with his business I had a free run of the German factory – it is this instance which he recollects in his book *From Beneath the Gallows and into Battle* (Paris 1980, p. 40):

> I must confess I did not expect this; in spite of this, I was not very surprised: 'Such things do happen,' I thought. By the way, for a Jew, these repeated trips to and from Kraków and Lwów and back again, and establishing contact with Jews who were also camp inmates was something like walking a tightrope. But did anything during those years not carry the same risk as a tightrope walker for an active Jew?

I do not think that the comparison with a tightrope walker is really appropriate. For an acrobat always has a safeguard, even during his most daring acts, namely, a discreetly stretched-out net below for protection in case he trips. All I had was a small tube with a cyanide crystal in case I tripped.

This was the end of my task and my contact with Boruchowicz. I accomplished that which I had set out to do. From then on comrades from the Polish Socialist Party would take over. However, I would like to add a few interesting details to do with this affair, namely, that the reader can find many different versions in Occupation Literature of how Boruchowicz was saved. For example, one of the most important activists in the

WITNESSES

Kraków Jewish Relief Council, Professor Tadeusz Seweryn, writes in the *Medical Survey* (1967, no. 1, p. 171)

> The person who initiated the transfer of some people from Lwów to Kraków was Adam Rysiewicz [Teodor], an outstanding socialist activist during the occupation, who, when he found out from the Kraków railwaymen that Maksymilian Boruchowicz, a talented writer and good organiser was in the Janowski Camp and was asking for help in escaping this torment, asked Władysław Wójcik to go to Lwów and to prepare a plan for getting Max out and for bringing him to Kraków. When Wójcik had discharged his duty, the contact, Józefa Rysińska [Ziutka] went to Lwów and handed over documents in the name of Michał Borucki (a railway assistant) to 'Michał' and then, she brought him to Kraków. Wójcik met him at the Main Railway Station and he spent the night at his mother's house.

The beginning of the first sentence and Ziutka's name as a contact are the only true details to be found in this account. The rest is fantasy based on gossip and unconfirmed guesses. Władysław Wójcik never once travelled to Lwów for the sake of Borwicz (Michael Borwicz is Boruchowicz's post-war name) and saw him for the very first time in the Kraków railway station.

Another 'historian' from the occupation period, Paweł Lisiewicz, gives a yet more interesting version in W. Bartoszewski's book *This One is From My Country* (Kraków 1966, 1st edition, p. 119)

> During the early period, the Kraków Jewish Relief Council and the District Committee of the Polish Socialist Party initiated help to Jews (mainly a work camp on Janowska Street). In addition to J. Cyrankiewicz, Z. Kłopotowski and Adam Rysiewicz, pseudonym 'Teodor', there was Lucjan Motyka, . . . who took part in saving Michał Borwicz.

This kind of nonsense went on for the simple reason that Borwicz himself made the true facts about his escape from the camp and my part in it available only in the last edition of the above mentioned book, *From Beneath the Gallows and into Battle.*

FUGITIVES FROM THE JANOWSKI CAMP

Borwicz's escape made further contact with the Janowski Camp possible right up to the time of its liquidation in November 1943. Amongst the escapees was Janka Hescheles, the orphaned daughter of Henryk Hescheles, the editor of the *Moment* who perished at the hands of Ukrainians during a massacre of Lwów Jews during the early days of the German occupation. Janka's mother was murdered in Piaski among a group of ambulance doctors. Ziutka Rysińska brought Janka to Kraków and I took the girl to our flat in Dębniki. She spent several days with us, after which Wanda Janowski, the future Mrs Wójcik, took her to her house. Janka stayed with her for several months and after that there was more wandering about. But all this happened in 1944 when I was already in Hungary. Miriam will write about this in more detail.

After leaving the camp, Janka describes the moment of her arrival in Kraków in her diary as follows:

> Mrs Rysiewicz took me to Mr Piotrowski. I felt as if I had just regained consciousness and did not know where I am. I could hardly believe that I was actually going to bed in a silent room and no-one would disturb me.

The little fugitive from the death camp thought she was free. But many long months of danger and wandering awaited her, which we, who were sharing her fate, also had to live through.

6

COUNCIL FOR JEWISH AID ('ŻEGOTA') IN KRAKÓW: FIRST STEPS

MIRIAM

According to official data found in many works about the Jewish Relief Council, the organisation was formed in Warsaw in December 1942, following many attempts at different types of individual aid from Polish and Jewish underground activists. The Kraków branch was called into being by Marek Arczyński, the secretary of the Warsaw Council, in April 1943.

In my memoirs, or rather fragments of memoirs which were written back in the fifties, spring of 1943 figures as the time of my nomination for the representative of Jewish society in the Kraków Council. However, after looking through the documents and notes which survived from the time of the occupation, it appears that this happened somewhat later, probably during early summer. I do not remember the exact date, but instead I clearly remember how I found out about the formation of this organisation.

One day I heard from Dr Helena Szlapak that Adam Rysiewicz would like to see me that very evening. As usual we met at Dr Szlapak's house after surgery hours. As was his habit, 'Teodor' curtly informed me that such a post had been created and immediately afterwards added, 'Don't ask about any details, these you will find out about from someone else. They asked me in Warsaw to include at least one Jewish member in the organisation. All important Kraków Zionists either have already been liquidated, are incarcerated in Płaszów or maybe in hiding somewhere. I have no contacts with them. Then I thought of you. Surely, you could provide proof of some sort of Zionist past, couldn't you?'

COUNCIL FOR JEWISH AID

'Not really,' I replied truthfully.

'But before the war you used to work on the *New Journal*, and that used to be a Zionist periodical.'

'Yes, but I didn't belong to any party, and all I did in that paper was to edit the children's supplement.'

'That's all!' Teodor was outraged. 'Are you going to deny that you edited a periodical for Jewish children in the socialist spirit and say that it was not a left Zionist paper.'

'Of course not, but I never belonged to any Zionist organisation.'

'It would be better if you didn't talk such nonsense', he chided me. 'Actually, to tell the truth you didn't belong to the Polish Socialist Party either, and I am not at all sure how good a socialist you are – a lady to the manner born. But your work is not bad and you have your connections by now and that means a lot. Well, do you feel Jewish enough to join such an organisation? '

'Don't go on,' I said reluctantly.

This sufficed and he immediately dropped his ironical tone with me. What would it involve? It would be necessary to attend meetings and he would be prepared to help and to give advice in certain cases. In any case, I could see for myself. And he gave me an address of a technical office at 11 Jagiellońska Street where I was to go and see Stanisław Dobrowolski.

On the day, the day when I first went there, the heavy gates opened, albeit only a crack, and a tiny pale glimmer of hope penetrated into the interior. It was late, far too late, but for those who were still alive and struggling with their bitter fate, it was the last resource, the proverbial straw to which the drowning man clings. But it was not just a straw, but a fraternal hand stretched out in aid.

I was the only one for whom the meeting I attended was the first encounter with these people. I was to work with them right up to the end of the war. It seems that before I joined the Council, several such meetings had already taken place, as I heard details of various rescue operations and names of various charges – as the Council's Jewish clients were called – were mentioned. The main point under discussion was the question of the insufficient funds allowed the Kraków branch by the central Warsaw office. Regardless, I was given the task of finding Jews in need of help.

In all accounts about the activities of the Jewish Relief

Council, two points recur most frequently, namely the recruitment of people prepared to take part in rescue operations, both Poles and Jews, and the raising of funds. Not many accounts describing the recruitment of the charges themselves from the Kraków area exist. A lot has been and is being written on this subject in works concerned with the central Warsaw Council. In Warsaw the situation was quite different, with a much larger group of workers, with many Jewish party and social activists among them and a large number of ghetto fugitives who had contacts with these activists and who, after receiving initial help themselves, supplied the Council with new clients by the chain system. The story about Jews hiding in Kraków I can relate, drawing on my own experience. But before I describe this work which was completely different from my previous conspiratorial activity, I would like to reminisce about the people who comprised the membership of the Kraków Jewish Relief Council.

Firstly, a bit about the one to whom 'Teodor' sent me, the Chairman of the Kraków Council, Stanisław Dobrowolski, pseudonym 'Staniewski'. I got in touch with him even before he invited me to the first meeting. He was a pleasant young man, and so calm and controlled, that one felt secure and safe as soon as he came into the office on Jagiellońska Street. In those days this was nothing more than illusion, but it had a good influence on morale and this in itself was a great achievement. I never knew and to this day I still don't know what the official function of this office was. I only remember that there were three clerks, one of them a girl. They must all have been initiated, because in addition to the meetings which were held after closing hours, I often dropped in during the day in order to report on various matters, and the other contacts did the same. It was obvious that we were not coming to the offices as clients. Dobrowolski was my godfather, as it was he who chose the pseudonym 'Mariańska' to be used in the Council for me. This name stuck to me to such an extent that it has remained my second surname to this day. Dobrowolski represented the Polish Socialist Party. He made everything he had available to the Council; his office, various contacts and his tireless toil, even though, after all, 'Żegota' was only a part of his conspiratorial work.

The organisation's treasurer was Anna Dobrowolska (no

COUNCIL FOR JEWISH AID

relation), known here as 'Michalska' who was a teacher by profession. She lived on Wielopole Street. To this day I remember the dark gateway and worn steps of this house, and the tall, slim figure of Mrs Dobrowolska, her kind eyes behind spectacles and the Council account books which she kept so carefully and scrupulously as if they were not the dangerous documents they were, but rather some innocent statements relating to pre-war social insurance premiums. At the beginning, for the sake of security, she used to hide these notebooks somewhere on the balcony under the coal chest (coal chests in those days were virtual treasure chests of secrets).

But in time, as the numbers of financial statements and receipts signed by the charges with real surnames increased, she simply used to take them out of the wardrobe in her room. I think that she did not even try to push them into a dark corner. I took some of these receipts from the year 1944 to my own hiding place, also in a coal chest, and I have kept them to this day.

For the sake of camouflage, we decided at one of the meetings, that every sum paid out to Jews would be written down as being a hundred times smaller (i.e. 10 instead of 1000), both on the receipts and on the statements and the dates as ten years back. This was very naive. Besides, not all the contacts and charges used this code as can be seen from the documents published here. On many receipts the Council secretary would write various comments, such as 'The Camps' or simply, 'Płaszów', etc.

'And what will you say', I questioned Mrs Dobrowolska, 'if they should ask where you, a Polish teacher, got all these Jewish names from, and especially as the ink is fresh?'

'No one will ask. Don't even think such thoughts', she castigated me. Actually, luckily, no one did ask.

After the war I realised how important was the order from the Warsaw Central Office that the recipients of money should sign the receipts with their real names. This in no way endangered the majority of them, as by then they were known by a different, Aryan name. It could only be dangerous for those who had been put in Płaszów. I came to the conclusion that those Jews who received help but did not know where it came from, often made light of the Council's work. I felt a great deal of satisfaction when I was able to show such a critic a receipt carrying his own signature. And this happened more than once.

In the Council, Anna Dobrowolska represented the Democratic Party. There was another Council member from the same party, the painter Janusz Strzałecki, whom I mistakenly described in my unpublished memoirs as belonging to the Communist Party. There was no representative of that party in the Kraków Council.

The third person – from the point of view of so-called party representation – was Professor Tadeusz Seweryn, member of the Peasant Party and ethnographer. He worked under the pseudonym 'Socha'. He was the deputy of the Polish delegate of the Emigration Ministry and Director of Civil Conflict. He was also a member of the Underground Court which gave out death sentences to collaborators and informers who tracked down members of the Polish underground, Jews in hiding and their protectors. 'Socha' made available to the Kraków 'Żegota' a military shortwave set for broadcasting abroad. I personally transmitted a telegram to the leadership of Jewish organisations, signed by Stefan Grajek and Józef Sak after the Warsaw uprising. The handwritten text of this telegram forms part of our private archive. Tadeusz Seweryn's attitude to Jewish affairs had a certain solemn, even professional quality. But behind this controlled stance and apparent stiffness, there was a very human and noble heart. While he never mentioned it during all the years of our collaboration, it was after the war that he told me how hurt he had felt when during the meetings, where technical, clerical and other 'normal' matters were being discussed, I would smile bitterly, as these must have seemed to me to be far removed from the everyday Jewish lot. I am not sure if it really was like that. We both worked on the Committee of Auditors and we used to meet at the treasurer 'Michalska's' house and this is why my signature, in addition to the names of contacts who distributed the money, appears on many of the receipts.

The next, and actually the most important, Council member was its secretary Władysław Wójcik, also from the Polish Socialist Party, who used several pseudonyms, among them 'Czerski', 'Żegota' and 'Żegocinski'. The two latter ones had no connection with the name used by the Council for Jewish Relief. Wójcik had used these names before the formation of

COUNCIL FOR JEWISH AID

this organisation. It was quite simply a question of coincidence; his family came from a village near Kraków, called Żegota. Wójcik held all the contact strings. Both my Mordecai and I worked with him, Mordecai until he left for Hungary and I until the end of the war, chiefly from that time onwards when the legitimation job of producing all sorts of documents became my direct responsibility. The legitimation office served both the Council for Jewish Relief and the underground Polish Socialist Party and was sponsored by Wanda Janowska, later Wójcik. But this subject is too extensive for it to be mentioned in passing.

Another person who was part of the Council presidium was Jerzy Matus from the Peasant Party, but one would rarely see him attending the meetings, his activities were mainly in the field, and he was in charge of a certain number of Jews hiding in villages. (I do not have any detailed information on this subject.)

The subject discussed at the first meeting in which I took part was the 'sorry' state of the finances, considering the requirements. At that time I did not have any information about the Council's funds or where they came from; in time I became familiar with these matters. I did not ask many questions, but listened to the reports of other members of the Council and to the details on the subject of the charges.

It did not take long for me to assess the situation. These kinds of problems were not new to me. The new element was that now we could help Jews not only by supplying them with documents – which we had been doing all along through the mediation of Kłopotowski and 'Teodor' – but we would be able to give them financial assistance as well. At the beginning this consisted of 300 złotys per month. When compared with the price of food and other basic commodities, this sum was negligible. But the very fact of the existence of such an organisation and the contact with people who had agreed to undertake such an operation, was more important for these survivors of the extermination than mere material support.

This small grant was also important for us personally. In the summer of 1943 we found ourselves in a very difficult situation. After Kłopotowski's arrest, the whole bread business, which we had been obtaining using false food ration cards, collapsed and we were finally forced to sell anything of value, however little there was. During this period in Kraków I had to look after my small niece and her father, who had been rescued from the Dębica work camp by Ziutka Rysińska. He was living with her aunt where we had to pay and where, despite this, we had no assurance of his safety. My gardening work in Bronowice which, so far as possible, I carried on with through the summer and autumn, produced very modest rewards, even including a supply of fruit and vegetables, thanks to my friend Janka. So, the small grants from the Relief Council did provide some relief.

As soon as I familiarised myself with the programme and the demands of the Council, I set to work. It was necessary to reach the Jews in hiding, to establish contacts and to supply them with financial aid, presently limited in scope, and with the appropriate documents.

My cousin Mituśka Hochberg was drawn into this work almost automatically. She set to work with great enthusiasm, and almost immediately she reported the first charges. She had connections with the Madritsch Company and she knew many Jews who were in the Płaszów Camp or who were hiding on the Aryan side at this time. She also looked after her elder sister Hela and her brother Zygmunt who, like Mordecai, was not in hiding but was involved in trade and had good contacts with Germans like Madritsch and Tisch. The Germans did not let the grass grow under their feet and while providing help to Jews in Płaszów and affiliated camps they stocked up with dollars, using Zygmunt as a contact for these illegal transactions. A number of the grant receipts have 'via Mituśka' or 'via Niuśka' written on them – which means via Niuśka Mehl, who was a brave Jewish contact for the Kraków Council.

Mituśka organised an 'office' for us in the flat of the solicitor Jan Wcisło on Starowiślna Street. A typewriter on which Mituśka tapped out reports and bulletins supplied by Wójcik and Dobrowolski was installed there. This copy had to do not only with Jewish affairs, but was also connected with the activities of the Polish Socialist Party. The secret receptacle for all the documents, copy and writing implements was the coal chest which was kept in the kitchen. These were – as I mentioned above – classic hiding places, and this one in the Wcisło household passed the test a lot later on, that is after the Warsaw uprising in the autumn of 1944. This happened after both Wcisłos had been arrested. The secret receptacle was full of dangerous documents, including completed identity cards for Warsaw Council workers. The Bund (Jewish Workers' Party)

COUNCIL FOR JEWISH AID

contact, Inka Schweiger, came from Milanówek to pick them up, but before they could be given to her, the Wcisłos were arrested. We had no idea why, and were anxious about the possibility of the hiding place being discovered.

Wójcik organised a foray into the flat. Three of us went in: Mituśka who had the keys, Wójcik and I. The stairs were guarded by 'Zocha', i.e. Jadwiga Rysiewicz, 'Teodor's' sister, along with another Polish girl whose name I don't remember – both armed with revolvers; Wanda Janowska stood guard in the gateway on the opposite side in order to be able to signal to the two girls in case anybody suspicious appeared. Everything happened very quickly and efficiently without the need to use the arms. The secret place had not been discovered, despite the fact that the flat was in a state of typical post house search disorder, with everything topsy-turvy. We took the copy, and the ID cards departed for Milanówek the next day. It is easy to tell this story, but somehow the thought comes to mind, what if we had not succeeded in this undertaking, then, certainly, I would not be now sitting at my typewriter in order to describe this small episode, one of many successfully completed.

Now a few words about coal chests. We got to know one such secret receptacle quite early on in our work, in the Krajewski flat on Skawińska Street. A duplicating machine was placed under a layer of coal and it was used for the printing of the underground press. The chest had a false bottom and one of the walls was removable. We used this idea when we built – much later on – the next two, namely the one on Starowiślna Street and another, identical one, in 'my room' in Wanda's flat on Wrzesińska Street, where, for most purposes, I lived right up to the end, that is until the liberation of Kraków. Wanda's brother Władysław Janowski made both of them and painted them a flaunting red. Both in summer and in winter they were loaded with coal from above and from below . . . with danger. But they served their purpose. I would also like to explain where the wooden boards used to build them with came from: beautifully planed, of just the right thickness and width, as they were. (I wonder whether such details will add value to our memoirs. If so, what sort of value? Literary? Historical? Although I have come to the conclusion that even such a tiny detail can in some, perhaps a thousandth, part explain those five years of our life: nearly two thousand days, many thousands of hours, divided into hundreds of thousands of minutes. So, I think perhaps it is after all worth while to write about it.)

It was in Dr Helena Szlapak's house, who always took an active part in many of our experiences and enterprises and continues to live in our hearts to this day, it was there that I met one of the directors of the Alcohol Monopoly – I cannot recall his name – and I mentioned in his presence that I was looking for some dry and well planed boards.

'Why? For what purpose?' he asked.

'We need two coal chests in order to stock up for the winter', I said, winking imperceptibly.

He asked no further questions, but announced his readiness to supply us with such boards. I gave him the dimensions and described the approximate amount of wood that would be needed. Let this man and those boards also enter the pages of the history of the occupation years and of our work.

During the first few months of our work in the Council, Mordecai and I handled the affairs passed on to us by Dobrowolski, Wójcik and 'Teodor'. My part in the Council meetings probably constituted the smallest part of my work. The clearest expression of this is the following fragment of a letter I wrote to Dr Berman: 'one thing I can tell you, and that is that however the problem of "attending meetings" was always difficult for me, so my work for the firm is for me always the first and most essential goal.' The firm – as can easily be guessed – was a cryptonym for the Relief Council. I received the original of this letter in Israel from the late Dr Berman a few months before his death.

Before our legitimation office was transferred to Wanda Janowska's new flat on Wrzesińska Street, it had been located in her old place in Podgórze. The difficulty lay in the fact that no one besides me had access to it. This fact made our work more difficult and complicated. At that time our main 'postbox' was – and actually remained so to the very end – Dr Szlapak's flat on Garbarska Street. Her pseudonym 'Garbarska', taken from the street name, also appears on some of the receipts from the grant recipients. She looked after several people whose names sometimes appear on the receipts, among them: Drobnerowa (probably the sister-in-law or the wife of Bolesław Drobner's nephew), Rela Schneider, an engineer, and her mother, Helena Molnicka, and two children whose names are not mentioned. As the

COUNCIL FOR JEWISH AID

doctor had a private gynaecological practice at home in addition to her work in the Health Clinic, it was a very good place for women to meet. But what was to be done, as men frequently had to be there as well? At the beginning of the war we used to meet there with Cyrankiewicz, and after his arrest, very often with 'Teodor', and he also used it as a meeting place with other comrades involved with conspiratorial activities. Marynia, Dr Szlapak's trustworthy housekeeper, used to say that such were the times that nowadays even men had to consult a gynaecologist. She was, of course, joking, as she knew very well what was going on in the flat. If one of us came into the waiting room, sometimes filled with real patients, she would open the door to the little drawing room and would say, 'The doctor would like you to wait in here, please'.

It got to the stage where I would deposit a packet of ID cards for the contact on the sideboard in this drawing room – or the opposite would happen, where one of our girls would leave some necessary papers for me – and all this without the doctor's knowledge as she was busy in the surgery. Sometimes the scenario looked like this: Dr Szlapak would burst into the room, just to see me for an instant.

'Has Baśka been?' I would ask. 'Has she left something for me?'

'No, I don't think so, as I haven't seen her.'

At that stage, without saying anything, I would reach up to the top of the sideboard, and take down the envelope I had been expecting.

'My dear,' Dr Szlapak would say, 'it would be nice to know what is going on in my own house, so I could at least hide something away if necessary.' But she never uttered a word of protest or gave any sign of displeasure. On numerous occasions she would act as a contact between Mordecai and me, when we would be returning from the field and would not have seen one another for several days. She was our guardian angel, our friend, adviser in difficult times and she organised medical help for sick charges as she knew doctors whom one could trust, and she would take upon herself the grave responsibility of placing 'Aryan' patients with forged papers in hospital.

When in the summer of 1944 the Germans mobilised Poles for the digging of trenches and one needed a really serious medical certificate to be excused from this forced labour,

Dr Szlapak organised such a certificate for me. According to her I was a victim of active consumption, and it included an X-ray of badly affected lungs, a blood sedimentation lab report and something else which I do not remember. Armed with these certificates which were forged from beginning to end, I presented myself in front of the German commission and I was pronounced officially exempt from the trench digging work until 20 October 1944: 'Zur Schanzarbeit bis 20.X.44 untauglich', with a seal of the crow and Commissar Walther's signature. By October I was no longer worried about an extension of the certificate, as by then German administration was in such a state of chaos, that I gave no further thought to any forced labour, and in any case the Germans got nothing out of their trenches, as the Soviet tanks were not stopped by them for even one moment. While standing in a long queue in a crowd of people to get the exemption certificate I overheard certain conversations which convinced me how wrong we had been in our evaluation of the state of the war at that time. Like others, I, too, had believed that by October the Soviet troops would have long since gone beyond Kraków. Every person who emerged carrying an exemption for the next few months, would exchange an ironical smile with those still in the queue and would whisper, 'By then, what might not happen . . . !' We were certain that there would be no more Krauts by then. In the meantime the Red Army offensive halted somewhere near Rzeszów and did not move forward again until January 1945.

The seal and the commissar's signature served as a model for our brilliant designer Edyś Kubiczek. He immediately produced an identical seal and he forged the commissar's signature so well, that Walther himself would not have been able to tell it apart. On one occasion Edyś carried out an experiment on us. He asked three of us to write our signatures on a piece of paper and then he signed our names as well. It turned out that none of us were able to recognise our own signature.

Two women whom I met at Dr Szlapak's house left a deep impression on my life and work during the occupation. One of them was Maria Hrabykowa, called Dzurzyńska after the war, who worked in the Labour Office. She was such a perfect office administrator that her German boss ended up trusting her completely. She was in charge of – if my memory does not deceive me – the work section of Polish workers, the register of all those sent to work in Germany. She maintained that if her boss, God forbid, decided to check one of the secret drawers in her desk, she would come to a sticky end. She was so well-respected in the Labour Office that she was able to fix anything possible, or rather impossible, in any other department. After we met, I used to obtain all sorts of work certificates with fictitious names for our charges, but these certificates were perfectly legal and were incorporated into the official register. In some cases, she was able to get Poles, who had been sent to forced labour in the Reich, back home. At one stage I managed, with her help, to get a work card for Władysław Woźnik, a well-known dramatic actor in the Słowacki Theatre in Kraków. At the time I had a strange feeling – something akin to pride, that it was I, a Jewess, who was in a position to do something for a Polish actor. And this was not an isolated case. Just before the Soviet Army marched into Kraków, the Germans decided to issue new work cards in a new colour. In place of the yellow ones, they were now greyish-green and checkered. Mrs Hrabykowa went with me to the storeroom after office hours, opened an enormous parcel of the new forms and to start me off, gave me 200 of them. Both of us worried about all that work awaiting us before all this could again be filled out and stamped. But the worry was unfounded – two weeks later Kraków was liberated.

The other woman I met at Dr Szlapak's house was Teresa Lasocka, who became the wife of Professor Karol Estreicher after the war. In her official capacity she worked in the Central Care Council, which was a centre for helping Polish prisoners and their families. Her unofficial function was rather more important, as she maintained contacts with the camp at Auschwitz. She used the pseudonym 'Tell' and this signature appears on the letters, lists and news items cards to be found in the Auschwitz museum. Furtive notes from the camp were sent by Cyrankiewicz to her address and many of those who managed to escape from the camp with the aid of the camp's conspiratorial organisation which was directed, among others, by Cyrankiewicz were sent to her. It was from her hands – if one can express it this way – that the Council for Jewish Relief took over the care of the fugitive Szymon Zajdów, a Jew about whom more will be said later.

Teresa would receive documents required for her charges

from our legitimation office. For quite a long time we used to meet at Dr Szlapak's house, until one day she gave me her private address, which was a sign of great trust, which I valued greatly. Purely by chance, Teresa lived in the same house where Dobrowolski's office was located, the place where we all met and where the Council meetings were held, 11 Jagiellońska Street. We never brought up the subject of my Jewishness: it only occurred to her in quite exceptional circumstances. One day Teresa suggested that I go with her to the Liban Camp to distribute parcels among Polish prisoners. The camp got its name from the pre-war owner of the quarry in Płaszów. Most of the inmates there were young Poles who had run away from compulsory labour gangs or for different sorts of administrative offences, mostly for being caught in the streets after curfew hours. I remember once heading home just before nine o'clock and not being certain how accurate my watch was, so I asked a passer-by what time it was. 'Five minutes to Liban,' he replied. I knew what that meant.

I did go with Teresa to the camp. This happened a few days before Easter 1944. The prisoners were brought together into a large shed, where the priest led a mass for them. A crucifix was placed on a box covered with a dirty piece of tarpaulin and a tall, thin priest started to pray. The prisoners were sitting down in rows on benches made from boards resting on wooden blocks. They were coming in slowly, as many were chained in such a way that they were able to walk only using tiny steps, with some of them chained together in pairs and there were those who had an arm chained to a leg and, in addition, were dragging a ball and chain behind them. Those were the ones who had attempted to escape and had been caught. When they walked, the chains clanged. There was a young boy who cried throughout the prayers, a simple farm lad with his head shaved and his legs chained. It seemed to me that it was blood not tears dripping from his eyes. But what significance did this have when compared with the sea of blood in those times! I do not know why I cried along with him. By that time, it had become a rare occurrence in my case. And it was not as if I were crying on his account, for the sake of this one Polish boy. Right next door, in the Płaszów Camp, thousands of Jews were suffering and dying. I was not able to bring them parcels and no one led holiday prayers for them. They had to pray in secret and would die if they were caught doing it. It was not for this lad that I cried and not for the others sitting here chained like galley slaves. The world, this terrible world of human wickedness and crime, was all around us, it seemed like there was no end in sight. The tears, the prayers which the priest was mumbling in Latin seemed powerless. Maria Konopnicka's words which came to me from afar, from the past, kept racing through my mind, 'But the black cross stood motionless and silent on the table, like silent altars in the face of tears . . .'.

Suddenly Teresa nudged me with her elbow and I followed her glance: a large, white, fat louse was promenading along the black cassock of the priest and after a while it went in behind his collar.

'He must be told,' she whispered, 'he has just been listening to confessions from typhus patients.' Yes, the priest had to be warned. I stopped crying.

When we left the camp, for the first time Teresa asked about my family. 'I have no family.' That was all I said, but it seems that it was enough, as two days later Dr Szlapak told me that Teresa had asked her if I was Jewish.

'I told her I didn't know that, that I knew you before the war and that I never thought about it.'

This amounted to a diplomatic lie, but apparently it did not satisfy Teresa, as a few days later 'Teodor' brought up the same subject, using his own style, 'You should not blubber in front of other people. Teresa has asked me if you are Jewish. As it happens, in her case it is of no consequence, but why do it?'

'But it happened in a camp for Poles', I tried to defend myself.

'Yes, but it looks as if your tears were Jewish ones and Teresa found you out.'

'Teodor' was probably right, these tears were of a kind by which a Jew can be recognised. We never again discussed this subject and Teresa's attitude to me and to Jewish matters remained unchanged.

7

I DID NOT KEEP A DIARY
... SCRAPS OF MEMORIES

MORDECAI

I lost counts of my trips to Lwów. Each time I told myself, enough, but soon after, there I was again, with a new project and with new feeling of hope of, perhaps, being able to save at least one more person from the jaws of death.

I did not keep a diary, as the hand which held the pen would go numb from any words which could have expressed that which I saw. That which was committed to memory has remained there and cannot be erased. However, in the same way as I managed to save my German documents from the Niesel und Kämmer factory, a few scraps of paper and a handful of notes about those events also survived, beyond my expectations, and at one stage I thought to myself, if I die, they will also be lost. During certain periods I began to doubt that one single Jew would manage to come out alive from this inferno which I saw all around me, in order to give a true account of it. At that time we still believed that in the future, world justice would prevail and the criminals would be duly punished.

So, after returning to Kraków from yet another such trip I wrote down the following in January 1943:

> Three days ago the Jews did not come to work to the factory. Word went round that this meant that the camp was being liquidated [Janowski Camp]. I went up to Köller, the director, and asked him what the meaning of this was, did this mean the end of our group. He said that the camp commander had promised him personally that nothing was going to happen to them and they would

I DID NOT KEEP A DIARY . . . SCRAPS OF MEMORIES

come to work the next day. I went into town and walked on Janowska Street alongside the camp, but did not see a living soul. From time to time, Italian soldiers, dark-haired, Jewish looking, rode past on their motorcycles. I thought I detected fear in their eyes, shots could be heard. The following morning at six a.m. I went in a chauffeur-driven lorry belonging to the firm to pick up 'our' Jews. There were also a few Germans who had come to pick up their workers. These Germans either wore Wehrmacht uniforms or were civilians with swastikas in their lapels. We were all standing near the gate when suddenly a young SS officer went up to one of the waiting Germans, exchanging greetings; I was standing right next to them and heard what was said: he had not slept at all, as he had spent the night shooting Jews. He had to change his machine gun several times, because it was getting overheated and was burning his hands. I did not notice his rank, but I saw his face clearly as he was standing close enough for me to touch. A round face, protruding brown eyes, bloodshot from sleeplessness. The German to whom he was saying all this wanted to say something but could not do it, he twisted his mouth as if to smile, but this turned into a kind of strange grimace. I watched the SS man, his face rather good-natured, normal, almost friendly. It etched itself on my memory in such a way that even many years later I could have recognised him, this 'normal' murderer.

The next notation written down on a ragged notebook page is from June 1943. When I recollect now in what kind of mood it was written, I think I ought to have written these words with my own blood. I was deeply wounded and filled with horror, as if emerging from a nightmare. Words are inadequate and that which I wrote down at that time seems to pale against the reality of it.

I went to Lwów two days ago and I saw hell. Hell does not exist in the other world, hell is here on earth. The Lwów ghetto was burning. I stood there amongst a crowd of people – not people but among a mob watching a spectacle, like in the cinema. Is it possible that there were amongst them also people like me, but they kept silent like me?

Others cried excitedly, 'Now, now.' 'Yes, over there!' And then a man all on fire would fall from a house on fire. One uniformed German – I do not remember which uniform – caught hold of a running child and threw it straight in the fire, into the flames, a living child, a child. I was there together with a worker from the factory, half-German, half-Ukrainian. He pulled my arm and shouted, 'Let's get out of here!' He said something else as well, but I did not hear what. Could it be that he too was a human being?

This is how much I wrote down at the time and there is nothing more I can add now. The liquidation of the ghetto has been described by historians of the Holocaust and by people who managed to come out of hell alive. There are also statistics about how many Jews, men, women and children, died in this, so modestly named, action. But I am not familiar with the statistics. I always see that one child, only this one child.

8

NEW CONTACTS – NEW METHODS

MORDECAI

No more illusions remained after the liquidation of the Lwów ghetto – it may be that the Janowski Camp prisoners, or at least some of them, felt comforted by the thought that they were indispensable for the German war machine and that they would survive. I had thought for some time that I wanted to do something for Grubner, but he could not make the decision to escape. Instead, his eighteen-year-old elder daughter made the decision. She had a false identity card and looked like a German, blonde with blue eyes, and she also had an excellent knowledge of the language, as before the war she had lived in Bielsk and she attended a German grammar school. She had a lot of self-confidence. After she took on an 'Aryan' identity, her fate followed some strange turns. I am nearly certain that she is alive to this day, even though she has not kept up any contact with us after the war. But let us not get ahead of ourselves.

We arrived in Kraków late one evening after curfew, but I had no intention of staying at the railway station, where searches and documents checks were common. I took her to my flat on Starowiślna Street. I dodged around, we lurked in gateways and we managed to avoid the German patrols. Being stopped in the street at that time meant at best being sent to the Polish punishment camp in the quarry, and, more likely, straight to Auschwitz. We managed to reach the flat without incident and it was only here that everything became very complicated. My landlady opened the door and greeted me with the news that a 'blue' policeman had come to search my room and that he had left his address and that I was to report to him immediately on my return. What he had seen in my room was enough to finish me off. I found some suitcases in my room, I do not remember exactly how many, but there were quite a few. They contained a large part of the Birnbaums' clothing from Tarnów. A chauffeur, who had obviously been well paid by Litka's parents, had brought them during my absence. But that was not all: on the table there was an open postcard from Milek Frimerman, a seventeen-year-old boy from Tarnów, who was turning to me for help, as he heard that I was helping Jews: no more, no less. It was certain that the policeman had read the postcard and this in itself was enough to send me to the Gestapo. I had no idea how this Jewish boy found out about me, but I suppose that it must have been the Birnbaums who, seeing that I was able to move around freely and sure that I was in no danger, gave him my address. This amounted to thoughtlessness verging on stupidity, and I ended up having to pay for it dearly. It was only by a strange stroke of luck that I did not pay for it with my life. I was convinced that the policeman's visit was brought about by the pianist, a pre-war acquaintance of the Birnbaums where Litka had found temporary asylum. Everything pointed to blackmail. I made a decision to go and see this policeman the very next day. This decision, when I think about it now, was mad, but my actions at the time were full of such mad ideas.

Miriam insisted that she would come along with me and that she would wait for me in the street. The policeman called Bojko lived in the Podgórze district, on Krakowska Street, just past the bridge. I found him at home – it was after lunch. He demanded Miriam's address. If I was prepared to give it to him, then I could go home in peace. I did not know any Miriam. 'Have it your own way, in that case you will have to come with me where they have other ways of getting this address out of you.'

I made a snap decision, as I could see the situation was a lot more serious than I had anticipated. I took advantage of the instant during which he started putting on his shoes and bolted out into the street. Below the bridge I turned into a small side street and I jumped into the first available gateway. I only just managed to make a sign in Miriam's direction, indicating where I was. She waited for another minute and caught sight of the policeman, rather she guessed it was he, for he was running

NEW CONTACTS – NEW METHODS

and looking around in all directions along Krakowska Street, then she joined me in the gateway. A decision had to be made immediately. First of all I had to change my clothes, as I was wearing a blue jacket which attracted attention.

Trusting fate, I knocked on the first door I came to and it was opened by a concierge. I told her I had escaped from the Gestapo and that I was asking to be allowed in for a short while. She did not, for an instant, suspect me of that which could have been the most dangerous thing, namely of being a Jew. She was afraid to let me stay in the flat, so she took me down to the cellar. I was to wait down there until Miriam could bring me a change of clothing. There was no time to go to my flat in Dębniki, and I forbade Miriam to go there. She found another way, namely a friend of ours, a solicitor and his German wife, called Wcisło, lived near Starowiślna Street. We used to work in the same underground organisation; there was a secret receptacle for documents in their flat and communiqués of various sorts used to be copied there. From them Miriam managed to get a suitable jacket, a raincoat and a hat. When she returned, I was no longer in the cellar, but in the concierge's flat, where I had shaved off my very Aryan moustache. When I looked in the mirror after having put on my 'new skin', and especially after putting on the hat, I hardly recognised myself. I never knew the name of that concierge, but I have often thought of her with gratitude.

However, this was not yet the end of this dangerous adventure. It was obvious that I must, under no circumstances, return to the flat on Starowiślna Street; such an action would have been unforgivably foolish. As a result, all the Birnbaums' belongings, as well as all my own clothes and everyday articles were lost. But I was not prepared to give up this modest amount of property so easily: a few days later I went there to find out what was going on. I was greeted by my landlady in a state of terror; it was difficult to tell whether it was real or pretended. Without letting me inside, she shouted, 'Run for your life, the police have taken everything and they can return any minute to get you!'

There is no way of knowing what really did happen, but the fact remains that she helped herself to at least some of the things, as later I saw her in Wolnica Square, where all sorts of things and clothes were being sold. She was standing there, holding an armful of clothes, which certainly were the things which she had 'confiscated' from those suitcases. However, it was far too dangerous to try to recover them or to look for justice in this case. If one were ready to risk one's life then it would have to be for the sake of saving someone else's, and not for the sake of clothes. But I could not bring myself to give up the small packet of dollars which was hidden under the metal eaves outside the window of my room. This sum was all the cash we owned in the world. A few weeks later I went there again, and this time I did not allow myself to be frightened away. When the landlady opened the door, I pushed her aside without saying a word. I went into my room and with quick movement I opened the window. I took out the money and was going down the stairs before she had a chance to open her mouth to protest.

All I can add on the subject of Katia Grubner's strange fate, is that the next time I met her, I very nearly paid for it with my life yet again. She was a brave girl and she coped very well and there was no question of her ever going into hiding. She did spend a short time with us on Zielna Street in Dębniki. She found a job as a German stenographer and worked for a while in a trading company. But despite a lot of courage and nerve, she became somewhat frightened when some German from Bielsk recognised her there. 'I think that you are struggling a bit with your Aryan status', he said in jest one day.

Then Katia found a job in Skarżysko-Kamienna from a German newspaper advertisement. We heard nothing from her for a long time but she did send us her address. So, I wrote to her and said that I would visit her and gave the date, asking her to wait for me in the Skarżysko station. She did appear, but her expression was worried and she immediately warned me that she was not safe here, as in town she was being harassed by teenage street gangs who called her a 'yid'. I soon found out what it was like: we were followed by several such teenagers, until one of them brought along two German policemen. They stopped us and demanded our papers. Katia managed to whisper for me to cast loose from her, but it was too late. I could see what was coming, so I decided to show them my ID card, which, by the way, was authentic. It was possible to check up on it in the Kraków police station at any time, that is if they did not decide first of all to check up on other dangerous details which could immediately identify any Jewish man.

For one instant I thought that the end had come. In my imagination I saw a picture of how they would shoot me down and how I would fall face down in the mud, as it was a wet autumn day. This happened only for one instant, like in a dream, devoid of any logic, as the two belonged to the security police and would only take me away, not shoot me. They asked me what I had in common with the girl, and by this stage I was already quite calm. I said that I was asking her directions and that she wanted to show me which way I was supposed to go. They told me to go off. They took Katia with them. I took the next train back to Kraków, with the bitter feeling that all that effort to save this girl had come to nothing. But at the same time I had some hope that Katia would manage somehow. And in actual fact, she did, as she had good documents, and also it may well be that her personal charm had some effect as well, as she really was a charming girl.

MIRIAM

Unlike her cousin from Tarnów, Litka Birnbaum, Katia Grubner did not give up her struggle for life and she went about it independently, without being too much of a burden to us. After returning to Kraków, she again managed to find a job in some German office. From time to time she would visit us in Dębniki, always well dressed, perhaps even too loudly for a person in danger, but everything was in harmony and she did not awaken any suspicions. She was indeed very pretty, a natural blonde, with beautiful blue eyes, graceful and with a lot of self-confidence. She never took any interest in the fate of her father and younger sister who had remained in Lwów. Perhaps this was a form of self-defence and maybe, deep inside, she did suffer because of it, but she did not externalise her despair. She never brought the subject up.

Throughout 1944 when Mordecai had already gone abroad, she got in touch with me from time to time, until in the end, she confided the secret of her self-confidence and even a sort of light-heartedness to me, which was so unusual in a Jewish girl with Aryan papers. She had a German friend, a very handsome boy and a member of the German Philharmonic Orchestra. The Philharmonia, which was only partially made up of Poles, was active in Kraków and gave concerts in the city and on tour. I do not know how Katia came to meet this German. It appeared from her confession that he was in love with her, without, of course, realising that she was Jewish and he made this obvious to the Germans in the office where she worked. He would introduce her as his fiancée, and he even obtained permission for her to travel to Germany so he could introduce her to his parents. For this purpose she had to go to the Gestapo, where all documents necessary for the journey were got ready for her. This test did not frighten her as she was certain of her friend's protection, and she did actually take this journey. After this, she felt completely confident, to such an extent that when her German went away for a few days with the orchestra, she suggested that I should come to their flat to listen to an English radio broadcast.

When in the summer of 1944 a hurried evacuation from Kraków of German officials and their families began, from this pure German city according to Governor Frank, Katia, along with the Philharmonia and her German lover also disappeared without trace, with no word in parting. We are certain that she is living somewhere in Germany, mother to German children. Is she, and is it possible for her to be happy, this Jewess, whose family perished at the hands of German murderers? And do we really have the right to condemn her for the fact that she wanted to live at any cost? I have never been able to find an answer to that question. If one prefers, one can look upon all this as a romantic story. And what if the young German lover had known that Katia was Jewish, would he have left her? I cannot be sure of this either. To end this story, one must say that this desire to live in Katia's case in no way had any connection with collaboration with Germans or any resulting harm either to Jews or to Poles.

There were different ways of finding new contacts. Some of the addresses were given to me ready by Wójcik and Dobrowolski, but I had to use my own initiative to reach the majority of my charges. The first official contact postbox was the flat of the well known pre-war socialist activists Maria and Mieczysław Bobrowski, on Sebastian Street.

It was there that I got the Wieliczka contact, which in turn led me to another socialist activist, Józef Jedynak. He was one of the most wonderful underground people that I ever met. He was a retired miner, but he seemed to have some sort of special

NEW CONTACTS - NEW METHODS

rights so far as movement in the grounds of the salt mine was concerned, where Jews, that is Jewish slaves, were working at that time. His external appearance inspired respect and trust; he was a most splendid looking man. I came to respect his calm, sensible behaviour which was devoid of all fear, and his enduring commitment to helping Jews. Those few individuals who were in hiding in Wieliczka and who managed to survive, did so as a result of his influence on his party comrades, as he was the leader of the civil service for rescue operations. There was not a trace of what is called 'philo-semitism' in his relationship to Jews, as he simply did not acknowledge the existence of anti-semitism. I am not even sure if he was aware of the concept of humanism, but he was a humanist of the highest order. Both his daughters, Wanda and Józia, like him, were involved in underground work, especially Józia who was involved in Jewish affairs. Wanda was much more involved in general underground activities.

'Grandfather', for such was Jedynak's pseudonym, taught me how to give immediate help to Jewish 'surface' workers, that is, those not working in the mine itself. In the mine he himself used the following system: he dropped small, but steady amounts of money into the wagons laden with salt, when the guards were not looking. He also taught me how to include a small bank note of twenty or fifty złotys in cigarette and match boxes, and to throw them secretly into the ditches which the Jews were digging, for an unknown purpose, around the mine. I was, of course, not able to produce receipts for this money, but I got permission to do this from my Council colleagues. I was also allowed this privilege due to the great trust in which Jedynak was held by everyone. Perhaps someone who managed to hide such a box inside his coat is still alive somewhere and will read this account.

But much more important actions were arranged with Jedynak's help. It was he who put us in contact with four people who had found hiding places in Wieliczka. Three of them were hiding in a bunker in the Przetaczek family home. Once a month I used to go there carrying the Council's allowance. To this day we maintain the warmest relationship with two of them, Israel and Fryda. The fourth one was Maks Fischgrund, a Bund member, Salo Fischgrund's brother, who was living in Leon Palonka's house in Lednica Górna, a district of Wieliczka.

He had documents with the surname Misiołek, but he signed the letters, of which I received a large number, sent care of the Bobrowskis, in a different way every time, sometimes Feliks, other times Staszek. Fischgrund-Misiołek, owner of two names, was a very special client. He would ask me to do a myriad different things for him and he wrote me letters full of exclamation points and dramatic incantations. He was constantly plagued by all sorts of catastrophes. However, in spite of the fact that he was an extremely egocentric type, he was nevertheless involved in many very important affairs and without the slightest doubt, he genuinely cared for the fate of Jews who were in need of help. It might be of interest to cite various fragments, in order to illustrate the concept of the work into which we had been drawn and how we became entangled in its human, every-day aspects.

> Dear Mrs Mariańska! Would you please arrange for the filling out of the enclosed prescription. Will you please also send back the prescription as I need it all the time. Sorry to trouble you, but this medicine is and will continue to be unobtainable here.

> Dear Mrs Mariańska! The other day we sent a letter to you via Grandfather, in which we informed you that the shoes which you sent to Feliks are *too tight and slightly too short*. We ask you to send him a pair of *sturdier and a proper size 43* boots at your earliest convenience. The shoes which Feliks is sending back, are presently with Jadwiga and not with Grandfather. Why this is so, Feliks will tell you at the next opportunity, when you will be kind enough to reverse your stern decision, and visit Feliks again in a state of subdued anger.

> Dear Mrs Mariańska! I have been asked for help in connection with the compulsory evacuation of Warsaw. This is a matter which allows no delay. I therefore most urgently request for you *to visit me at your earliest convenience* preferably *immediately on receiving* this information. In my letter to Mieczysław Bobrowski I have asked him to thank you for arranging for the repair of the glasses and for the September allowance. Starting tomorrow I will begin

NEW CONTACTS - NEW METHODS

watching out of my window to see if someone is coming up the path.

A word of explanation: our Misiołek considered writing in the third person as amounting to a conspiratorial code. 'Grandfather' as I have already mentioned, was Jedynak. Jadwiga was Jadwiga Kruczkowska. She gave her support to my visit to Fischgrund and lent him some books from her marvellous library. She did not even hold my request against me, because she said that Fischgrund's appearance was very good. But this was not the only reason, as she herself was a brave and helpful person.

Władek Wójcik, who frequently picked these letters up from Bobrowski, would give them to me with the ironical comment, 'Here is another little love letter from Misiołek for you.'

But sometimes the letters concerned more important things and I must confess that they were not always about glasses, shoes or medicines. In December 1944 Bobrowski got another letter from Misiołek, which, for the sake of greater secrecy, this time was signed Staszek.

> My dear friends! I would like to inform Miriam *without delay* that the refugee who was in Bieżanów, has been evicted. He is temporarily to be found near Feliks, but will be evicted from there also *any time now* with all the ensuing *consequences* for such a gravely sick person. Would Miriam therefore drop in on Feliks *immediately* to sort this out. I wish to add that the evicted person has no personal documents of any kind. My dear friends! I am contacting Miriam through you in this instance, because I know that you belong to a *small group* (alas) of people who *disinterestedly* take the fate of their seriously ill compatriots to heart.

This 'gravely ill', 'evicted' person, if my memory does not deceive me, was a fugitive from the camp in Skarżysko, and his name was Jakub Mulner. His case concerns a person who deserves a somewhat broader treatment. One day, also through Jedynak, I met a handsome young man with the Aryan surname Jackowski, who was an official in the German subprefecture, the so-called *Kreishauptmannschaft*. This case was so extraordinary even in our very varied occupation experience, that to this day I find it quite astonishing how a Jew would have found the courage to take on such a position, without having such a totally Aryan appearance like we did. This man was the now famous Tel-Aviv lawyer Henryk Margulies.[1] I used to go and see him in the subprefecture and I would obtain various sorts of documents from him which could be used for Jews with Aryan papers and for Poles who were working in the underground. These were things like German certificates for inspectors for milk co-operatives and other economic posts, for people who would be able to move around more freely with such documents. I would receive forms, stamped and signed by a German official, and all that remained for me to do was to add the name of the supposed inspector and the place name. I used to carry these forms out just under the nose of the German gendarme guarding the gate, hiding them in the capacious pockets of my coat, which were deliberately torn in such a way that the papers immediately fell through inside the lining. In the winter I used skiing trousers tucked inside my boots for the same purpose.

We encountered great difficulties with filling out these forms, as one had to know the names of various villages around Kraków and we needed a suitable map. I told 'Jacek' – that is how Jackowski was known amongst his Polish colleagues in the office – about these problems. Without a second thought he went into his German boss's room and took down from the wall a small map with details of the surrounding country region. I can still see this scene as if it happened yesterday: the German raised his head from his papers and asked what the meaning of

---

[1] I was given the following information by Henryk Margulies's widow (he died in March 1984): he was born in Dąbrowa Tarnówska, and he obtained Aryan documents for himself and his mother during the occupation. With the help of a Polish school friend, Kowalski, he got a job in an amelioration office in Jędrzejow. He had to make an instant escape as a result of being denounced. He came to Kraków with very little cash in his pocket and no address. While wandering aimlessly through the streets he stumbled on the amelioration office. This happened after office hours. Seeing a light in one of the windows, he went inside. In an office he saw three Polish men sitting around a table. He introduced himself and said that he was an experienced amelioration worker and asked if, by any chance, there might be a job for him. The reply was surprising, 'At the moment we need a fourth for a game of bridge'. He was in luck, as he was an excellent bridge player. He played with them well into the night and managed to win not only a large sum of money, but also the sympathy of his partners. With their help he got a job in the office and since he had a good knowledge of German, he was soon promoted to being in charge of real estate and remained in this post till the end of the war.

NEW CONTACTS - NEW METHODS

all this was. Jackowski casually explained that he needed the map. When he got back to his room, he rolled it into a tight tube and put it into my torn pocket. There were many different examples of bravery in those days, and this gesture seemed to me to be an example of simple 'Jewish cheek', but how much it was appreciated.

Because of his position I was aware of the fact that Jackowski knew a lot of Polish officials in charge of the abandoned or requisitioned country houses, the so-called *Liegenschaften*. It was to him that I turned for help for the 'evicted' one. Within a few days he organised a farm worker's job on a farm near Kraków for this boy. It was up to me to make an ID card with a new name for him. This required two round trips to Wieliczka, first to get the photograph, then to fill out the document and so on, which were normal procedures in such a case. Everything went according to plan and Misiołek's next letter says, 'Early this morning, Janek together with P. set off for his new job, full of gratitude that you were able to make the arrangements so promptly, as well as for the things you sent, and for the 100 złotys . . .' [read: a thousand złotys].

When the boy had already arrived at his destination, I suddenly remembered that I had overlooked a certain detail, which was the first and only time this ever happened to me. In the rush, I had forgotten to fill out the space in the ID card relating to deregistration from a fictitious address. This would have meant that when the farm manager attempted to register the new worker in the local social security centre, the fact that the ID card was forged would immediately come to light. This could have tragic consequences for this Jew, as well as for the person who had recommended him, namely Jackowski. I rushed to him in a state of terror. He, however, behaved like a courageous fireman trying to save a person from a burning house. 'Bring me the stamp and the necessary details', he advised succinctly. 'I will take care of it.'

What if it is too late? - this thought preoccupied my mind as I ran to carry out his instructions. Luckily it was not too late. Jackowski wasted no time. He got on his bike and set off at a fast pace. He found the boy in the barn and managed to stamp the ID card and to add to it the required information in some dark corner and thus saved the situation: not just the situation; he saved a human being.

It was by then December 1944, not long before the end of the war, but the struggle to stay alive lasted to the very last day. I do not know and shall probably never find out if this camp fugitive remembers Jackowski and that incident. I have never forgotten it and I am passing on this apparently minor detail, which can be entered on the side of profits, namely one human life, among the statistics of losses amounting to millions, into the history of the Holocaust.

It is very difficult to maintain a chronological sequence in these memoirs. Some of the actions began in 1943, during the first year of our activities within the framework of the Council and they continued in 1944. We were involved in them to a greater or lesser extent up to the end of the war. For the present, lets concentrate on action connected with Wieliczka. Misiołek again speaks about my next charges in that town

> My dear Mrs Mariańska! Can you please drop in at the enclosed address as soon as possible. And bring a few złotys and a document from Mietek for the child. How is Wacek? Best regards, Feliks.

Mietek was Bobrowski and Wacek refers to Wacław Wojnarowicz, or Leopold Leinkram, about whom more later. Unfortunately I no longer recollect the names of the heroes of this affair, nor their address. This is most unfortunate, as the story itself, with which I became involved, is clearly etched in my memory. Two Jewish girls found shelter with a childless Polish couple. The elder one of the two, about eight years old, was Mundek Korn's daughter and it is about her that Misiołek writes in his letter. The other little one, only about two years old at that time, was called Krysia, but I am not sure if it was her real name. If I am not mistaken she had been entrusted to this family by her mother, Mrs Laufer, I think (I am not sure if this really was the woman's name). Now for an explanation why in his letter Misiołek mentions only one girl. The miner's wife who took the children over, concentrated all her maternal feeling on the little one. She herself obtained documents for her, naming her as the daughter of a deceased relative of hers, simply as if she had adopted her, albeit without official papers, but cherishing the hope that this child would remain with her. What did she base such a hope on? She never spoke of it openly as she was a sensitive and honest person and it must

NEW CONTACTS - NEW METHODS

have been difficult for her to express such an inhuman desire, namely that the mother, who had been resettled from the Płaszów camp, should never return. But every time I spoke to her, I felt that she was trying to convince herself of this. From a strictly logical point of view she was justified in this. She never had any communication from the mother, and all kinds of rumours circulated about the fate of those who had been resettled. 'Krysia belongs to me, to us', she said the first time I met her, and she repeated the same thing every time.

She categorically refused to accept any help whatsoever for this child, neither money nor clothing. The monthly allowance which she received was for the other girl, whom she also would introduce to her neighbours as an orphan given to her to care for by an orphanage. I spent many hours talking to this woman and always with the same goal in mind, namely to prepare her for and to warn her against the eventuality of the mother's return. I could see how blind and endless was her love for this child. The words I heard from her I never heard before from any other Polish woman who had been given Jewish children to care for. There, one would sense the feeling of threat, of continuous danger and of a shadow of death hanging over the whole family. She, on the other hand, would say that the child had brought happiness and warmth into her childless family. Even her husband, she told me, who liked to drink and would rarely come straight home after work, as he used to go to visit his friends, now, since the girl started living with them, spent every evening at home. On his day off, he would take the child for walks and he could spend hours playing with her. Krysia was beautiful and was always dressed up like a little doll. After a few months in this house, she no longer remembered her mother. In her childish voice she called them mummy and daddy.

'I shall never part with Krysia', the woman once told me. 'If it turns out that I have to give her back, I will go with them, wherever they may be, even if it means leaving my husband. If there is no other way out, I shall get a job as a servant.'

Soon after the end of the war Krysia's real mother tracked me down, probably with Misiołek's help, in the children's department of the Jewish Committee in Długa Street in Kraków. She arrived alone, looking happy and depressed at the same time. (A story like this one would make an excellent subject for a film and as a matter of fact, I have actually seen, after coming to Israel, a film about just such a child who had been 'repossessed' in Yugoslavia.)

'What am I to do? ' she asked. 'This is my only child, my husband is dead, I am all alone and the child does not want to know me. I go there every day and I bring her toys and sweets, but I do not know how I can buy her back.' This flood of tears, which should have been tears of happiness, turned out to be tears of woe. She did understand the feeling of the other woman, was deeply grateful to her and would do nothing to hurt her feelings, but she could not very well give up her own child. That day, when both of them arrived with the little girl, was for me a terrible ordeal. The child, grasping the arm of its second mother, was rejecting the tenderness of the real one.

'Please tell her,' begged the miner's wife, 'please tell us what to do. You know all about, you saw it all.'

I ended up having to be the judge in this case. I had no doubts whatsoever. The law, not only feeling, was on the mother's side. 'One needs patience', I said. 'You have to help each other. The child must return to its mother.'

I cannot remember how long the scene lasted, but in the end the Jewish mother came to say goodbye to me. She said that of all the terrible experiences in the camp, this was the most difficult one. The little girl agreed to go walking with her and from this walk she never returned to her 'mummy'. 'I have broken the heart of a woman who saved my child, but there was no other way out. Now I must try to leave Poland as quickly as possible. This will allow the wound to heal up faster.'

It did not, however, heal up all that fast. The miner's wife came to see me several more times. I talked her into adopting another child, as so many orphans of Polish parents remained in children's homes. In the end she took on a boy and she came to tell me about it. 'He is a nice child, but it is not the same as Krysia', she sighed. 'Krysia was mine and I cry for Krysia every single day.'

This story was not unique. After the war I was the witness of many such human dramas, so painful and unforgettable.

My next charges in Wieliczka were Marylka Aleksandrowicz, Dr Julian's wife, their son Jerzyk and a grandmother – I do not know whose. The three of them lived in a small room in a house

NEW CONTACTS - NEW METHODS

on the outskirts of town, but I don't remember the exact address. The conditions dictated by the family who was hiding them must have been quite hard, because the Council allowance was not adequate to cover it. By this time Dr Aleksandrowicz had already joined the partisans. Marylka struggled valiantly to find the necessary funds to keep them. But she did not accept my proposal of increasing the allowance when I suggested that I would try and arrange it. With the help of friends she sold everything still remaining from the things they had managed to save, but there was not a lot there. One of her letters which has survived in our archive is witness to her efforts. This is another small document which speaks between the lines about the unarmed struggle which was going on on the occupation battle field.

Wieliczka intermingled with our experiences in many strange ways, and I will return to this town again. In the meantime, throughout 1943, Mordecai and I used to go there to visit Jadwiga Kruczkowska, in order to be able, at least for a few hours, to forget about everyday duties and to breathe a different atmosphere which seemed to us like the pre-war variety, resembling a nice, friendly dream. Sometimes one would meet people whose very presence contradicted the threatening reality - Jadwiga and her sister Wanda were like this.

As I have already mentioned, I did not obtain all of my addresses from my colleagues in the Council. The consciousness that one was in a position to help people, and that means for this purpose were available, would constantly accompany me in my wanderings around the town. I attempted to make contacts using my instinct, but I must admit, not always successfully.

One day, while riding in a tram, I noticed two women, probably a mother and daughter judging by their appearance. They both seemed 'suspect' to me. Both were clearly depressed and it was their behaviour rather than their external appearance that indicated to me that they were Jewish, and of the unattached type without the possibility of refuge in a definite safe place. The elder one wanted to get off at the next stop. The younger one was trying to hold her back. I did not hear what she said, but it seemed that their journey did not have a goal and that it made no difference if they got off here or somewhere else. I got off along with them at the next stop and when they turned into a side street, I followed them. I started walking faster. 'Excuse me', I said, catching up with them.

They stopped.

We looked at one another for a few seconds, before I managed to blurt out, as my heart was in my throat, 'Is there anything I can do to help you? Perhaps you need . . .'

The younger one would not let me finish. In front of me I saw two pairs of terrified eyes and two faces blanched with fear. 'Why are you picking on us?' she shouted. 'What do you want from us? Leave us alone! . . .'

At that moment a passer-by turned and looked at us. There was a danger that this incident could have a completely different outcome from the one I intended and that I could be exposing these two women to immediate danger instead of helping them. I immediately turned around and went off in the opposite direction. I was devastated when I thought that these two people perhaps thought me a blackmailer and were probably glad that they got rid of me so easily. Where did they go? What was waiting for them at the end of that street and on many other streets along which they wandered, homeless and helpless? Who knows, and who will ever find out?

I had a similar experience with the little girl who used to bring flour, oats, mushrooms and apples to our flat on Zielna Street. She was about thirteen, was practically barefoot, wearing only some sort of wooden clogs, a torn scarf tied crosswise around her back and a faded, miserable little dress. A thin, freckled face and brown, red-rimmed eyes without a trace of a smile, like the eyes of a sick dog; for me this was enough. Polish country children never looked like this, not even when they came from a very poor family from a poverty-stricken village.

When she came the second time, carrying her wares, I started probing very gently. First, I bought as many wanted and unwanted goods as I could from her, then I gave her a plate of hot soup and I attempted, in an indifferent tone, to question her about less important things, like what her name was, where she lived, which village she came from, if she had parents and brothers and sisters. . . . She was so unwilling to speak, that I got not a single concrete answer to any of my questions. In the end I came straight out with it and asked her if she did not, by any chance, need some document, some paper, so the Germans

NEW CONTACTS - NEW METHODS

would leave her alone when she went around with her wares. With this question I completely cut off my road to her and she never came again. This confirmed that my suspicions had been right. I do not know what happened to this Jewish child who fought for her life with such courage. I felt helpless, as she managed to slip out of my grasp even though I could have done something for her.

I was not the only one who encountered such failures. 'Teodor' told me a story about how he twice saw a Jewish girl from his home town Sącz in the street in Kraków. Twice he tried to stop her, but both times she just ran away when he came near her. He felt very upset and disappointed because of this incident. Another time, as I was sitting with Dobrowolski in his office, a young woman carrying a box of goods came in (they were blocks of toilet soap). Stanisław whispered to me, 'A potential charge'.

'Very likely', I thought, but this time we did not even try to start a conversation - the central organisation was not a suitable place for it.

Not all my efforts were in vain, as in other circumstances I did manage to make contacts very successfully. I met in the street a woman I had known before the war, called Elza Matusowa. She was from Vienna, married to a Jew, who had embraced Judaism and was known in Kraków as a Jewess concerned with following Jewish traditions. She had been living in Kraków for many years and she had two children, a boy and a girl. I met her in the swimming pool in Krakówski Park: she was a keen sportswoman. I trusted her, and she was aware who I was. She told me how her husband and son had left Kraków at the start of war, and like many others had set off Eastwards. They kept in touch up to the outbreak of the German-Soviet war, and her husband sent her formal divorce papers in order to protect her. How was she managing to live? She was doing business with Germans; she had German suppliers in the Army, who were selling goods stolen from warehouses to her, primarily all kinds of drink and cigarettes. I showed her my hand and I said that I imagined that she must have some Jewish acquaintances as she had lived among them for many years. Then I told her that I was working for an aid organisation; she was overcome with joy. She immediately organised a meeting in her flat in Siemiradzka Street. This is how I managed to reach several persons who, from that point onwards, received an allowance and all kinds of required documents.

At Elza's house, first and foremost, I met Ania O. who has remained a dear friend of ours to this day. She was taking care of her whole family, including her mother, a sister who had a young daughter, and her own daughter and niece. Her brother and father had been shot by the Germans in Skała, where the whole family used to live before the war. At this time her sister-in-law was in the Płaszów camp. Ania was one of the bravest Jewish women I ever met during my work in the organisation. When we met, she found herself in a very difficult situation. All six of them, three women and three young girls, were in hiding in Ojców. Just at the time we met, they were forced to move out of there, because the house where they were hiding out in the loft had been requisitioned by German fliers. Ania found a new hiding place in Kraków, but had no money to pay for it. Anything of any value had already been sold and, quite simply, she was facing a catastrophe. But from the time of our meeting onwards, up to the end of the war, she received financial help and all necessary documents.

Ania, her mother and two girls moved to Grzegórzki, on the outskirts, to a house owned by a couple called Florek and Hanusia. She arranged for her sister and her daughter to stay in a potter's house in Dębniki. Payment was required in both places. Some of the receipts which are printed in the appendix bear witness to the amounts spent by the Kraków Council for Jewish Aid for this purpose. Ania also passed on money to other Jews in hiding. Receipts for these amounts can also be seen at the end of our memoirs. Right up to the end of the war Ania was convinced that I was Polish. I recollect one detail, which both of us remember to this day: at Christmas in 1944 I received a cream cake with a beautiful holiday greeting from her, which she obviously felt was owing to a Polish protector of Jews such as me!

Once I used her help, when a client finding himself under dire threat, had to be placed very urgently. This client was Szymon Zajdów, the pre-war Warsaw Communist who had escaped from Auschwitz. But a separate chapter will be devoted to this story. It was with Ania's help that we made contact with

NEW CONTACTS - NEW METHODS

the Lieberman family. Ten members of that family managed to find shelter in the cellar of the Home Army member Adam Kowalski after their escape from the Kraków ghetto. Hanusia, Florek's wife, had been a housemaid in the Lieberman household before the war and her connection with Ania led to contact being made with the people in hiding.

So it was that threads, fine threads of help, led from person to person, and these, in turn, were woven into nets which sometimes would enclose whole families of people in hiding or individual persons who were set up on the Aryan side. The history of any one of such groups or even of any one individual, forms a subject for a story. It is not possible to reproduce in a dry narrative the atmosphere of those years and this work, which continued for hundreds of days and nights. The fate of all the people connected with our work during the occupation is closely tied up with our own fate. The contacts made with people who, so to speak, passed through our hands, have been maintained to the present day, and even now every time we meet, we can spend hours reminiscing how it all happened. But many of our charges whom we knew personally, set off for different parts of the world and we lost contact with them, probably forever. But the others, and especially those who, like us, ended up in Israel, like us remember our common contemporary crossing of the Red Sea, the 'Hagada' of our time.

In Elza Matusowa's house I also met the wife of the famous Bund member Dr Joffe. I patiently allowed them to explain to me what sort of an organisation this Bund was, as in her eyes I passed for a Pole. It was not a bit funny, to have to sit opposite my persecuted brothers, under threat like the two of us, and pretend that we belonged to a higher race. But I agreed to do it for the sake of secrecy. Only in exceptional circumstances when I would lose all patience, would I come into the open. This would happen when one of the charges, who was in an identical situation to ours, that is, possessing good Aryan documents and able to move freely on the Aryan side, asked us to take care of some ordinary, everyday affairs for them. This mainly concerned women, who were always less vulnerable than men anyway. When one of them would say to me in her defence, 'But I am Jewish and I am well known in Kraków', I would briefly shed my Aryan skin and say, 'I, too, am Jewish and many Poles knew me here'. It was not so much a question of unwillingness, but of time which was carefully apportioned into hours rather than days. Sometimes, during the course of one day, I had to cross the town several times for very important and urgent reasons. Whenever I could, I avoided tram rides, as walking was safer.

Mrs Joffe brought a young Polish woman, Alicja Moskalska with her. She asked for financial support to be able to send parcels to a Jewish acquaintance who was a prisoner in the Płaszów camp and she had arranged for suitable contacts. This particular detail may not be of great importance, but a different, more important affair, showing how the different connections were made, is linked with Alicja's name. This young girl worked in a German forestry office (I do not remember the exact German name of this department). Again, in the same way as in the case of Jackowski, I took advantage of this acquaintance to obtain certificates for supposed forestry inspectors. Among others, I got such a certificate for Stefan Grajek from her, when after the Warsaw uprising he found himself in a group of Jewish underground activists in Suchedniów, a little town in the Kielce region. In one of Grajek's letters which is published here, the following request appears: 'I should like to ask you to try and get some sort of reasonable certificate for me, which would make my work easier.' It was just such a 'reasonable certificate' which I got from Alicja Moskalska. Marysia Sawicka, a permanent contact with the Warsaw group, mentions this document in her statement given in Yad Vashem in 1965

> Well, so far as documents are concerned, Stefan did have a document. I know, I remember. And it happened that in Kielce Stefan and I were walking [. . .] and we met some gendarmes in the street. And they stopped Stefan and called him over and he, of course, showed them this document and they saluted gallantly, clicked their heels and returned it to him.
>
> Well, it appears, that such a modest thing as a German certificate of a forestry inspector was more important than an ID card or a birth certificate.

To my great chagrin I did not, after the war, manage to make contact with Alicja Moskalska, who so courageously, under the very nose of her German boss, filled out and stamped

NEW CONTACTS – NEW METHODS

certificates, and put these completed documents for him to sign. She, too, like Maria Hrabykowa and Jackowski, was such a perfect and devoted worker, that her boss trusted her completely. I am at least glad that I remember her name and that it can be listed in our modest memoir along with those Polish people, to whom the life and safety of a hounded Jew was as important as their own.

Near Garbarska Street, next door to where Dr Helena Szlapak lived, I knew another Pole. This was Niewiara, a tailor whom I had known before the war as he used to work in Schornstein's, my cousin's husband's workshop. I knew that he was a socialist, a comrade of the Polish Socialist Party. I thought about him and his possible contacts with Jews. My intuition proved to be right. During my first visit he arranged for me to meet a 'certain Jewess'. I now give the floor to this lady, who at that time was a young girl, whose statement, deposited in May 1959, I found in the Yad Vashem archive. Genia Nussbaum, born Bornstein, recounts our meeting in the following way.

> [. . .] After many adventures, I got in touch with two of my friends who were in the same situation as I, that is homeless, and we began to look for some hiding place together. They were Hanka Weksler and Stefa Friedman, the latter also had a three-year-old daughter. In late 1943 we finally found shelter in the house of the concierge on 43 Czarnowiejska Street.
> [. . .] At the beginning all four of us were living in a bunker in the garden, in actual fact it was a potato store hole which had been widened a little, but when this temporary bunker collapsed, we moved to a little corner in the cellar. This second hiding place, in turn, did not seem safe enough, which resulted in our having to move again to a little corner in the loft. The entrance to this had a sliding trap door which our hostess slid open three times a day to pass us our food or to let me or Stefa out, as one or the other of us would go out in case of need.
> [. . .] Three women and child, hidden under the ceiling in a Polish house, we had, in addition to the continuous threat of being discovered by the Germans, other worries and problems which were difficult to find a solution for.

The most basic of these problems was how to pay, where to find the means to reward the hospitality of the Poles. The hosts were poor people, and had no income of their own and they were living primarily on the money we paid them as a monthly salary. This salary was not really very high, when one takes the current price of food at that time into consideration. For example, a loaf of bread cost 50 złotys, and naturally we had no ration cards. Everything had to be bought on the black market. Together with all our other requirements we needed seven thousand złotys a month. In addition to bread and potatoes, we got a warm dinner every day, including soup, oats and vegetables and a pint of milk a day for the child.

However, where were we to find those thousands? During the first few months things were not quite so difficult. We were selling off all our jewellery piece by piece and luckily we had had quite a bit of it. When this source dried up, we started selling our clothes, until we literally had nothing except what we were wearing.

Work was also a source of income and we knitted. We had quite a few trustworthy Polish acquaintances and they supplied us with wool for knitting and all sorts of alterations. This work not only proved a source of income, but also gave us something to do, which had a positive effect on the morale of people, like us, who were locked up in a tiny cell for over a year. This income, however, could not provide even a hundredth part of the amount necessary to pay our hosts, and this is why we decided to ask our Polish friends for a loan. After all, the end of the war was near. The Russians were not far away. This was after the Warsaw uprising, which means it must have been in August or September 1944.

Among others, I turned to Mr Niewiara, whom I knew to have been a socialist before the war and who, I knew, had been well disposed to my family, as he had worked in my father's workshop for many years until he got his master's diploma. Mr Niewiara received me in a very cool manner and could not wait for me to leave. When I asked for a loan, I got no answer at all. Crestfallen, I returned home empty-handed.

A week after my hopes had been dashed, we remembered

NEW CONTACTS - NEW METHODS

that Stefa still had a packet of unstamped pre-war hundred złoty notes. I decided to try my luck with Mr Niewiara once again, and this time instead of trying to appeal to his feelings, to offer him a business deal, the sale of unstamped hundred złoty notes. This time my reception was totally different. In a cordial and friendly manner, immediately Niewiara pressed 400 złotys which were all ready and waiting for me, into my hand, as of course during my previous visit shocked by the reception I got, I did not leave my address. He also explained the reason for his earlier behaviour, namely, that his flat was being used as the nucleus of the Polish opposition movement, and I happened to have arrived at a time when he had been expected an SS man to arrive at any moment for a fitting. Clearly, if he had seen me and if he had become suspicious because of my semitic appearance, it could have meant the end not only of me, but of Mr Niewiara and his 'tainted' flat as well.

This second visit took place on a Wednesday, and, of course, I do not remember the date. Niewiara asked me to come back and see him again on Saturday, where I would meet a certain young lady who would undertake to look after us. 'All your money problems will end now, as this lady will take you under her wing', Niewiara assured me. I returned to my cell in the loft in high spirits. Unfortunately, this mood disappeared very quickly after my return after I reported what happened to my cohabitants. They declared that it was bound to be a trap, and that, for sure, the Gestapo would be waiting for me instead of the mysterious 'good lady'.

However, I did go on Saturday. At five o'clock, in Mr Niewiara's sitting room, I first met Marysia (as I found out after the war, she was called Mrs Hochberg-Mariańska). The tall, handsome blonde threw up her hands in despair when she saw me, 'My dear, with your appearance you can't go around in the open'.

First of all I had to give her a promise that after I started receiving the monthly allowance, I would give up all my other business in town and that I would venture out only once a month for my meeting with her in Mr Niewiara's house. The next question concerned the amount of money we were paying our hostess for feeding and keeping our group. From that time onwards, every month, I regularly received seven thousand złotys from Mrs Mariańska. Mrs Mariańska did not make note of our address for the sake of security.

During my next few visits, Mr Niewiara supplied me with certain bits of information pertaining to Mrs Mariańska. She had a vegetable business and used this as a cover to be able to move freely around town using a cart and horse laden with vegetables. Inside the sacks of potatoes and onions, money and documents and clothing were hidden for her charges of which she had very many – Dr Aleksandrowicz and family, among others. She also obtained documents for us, namely Polish ID cards for the women and a christening certificate for the child.

Our last meeting took place three days before the Russians arrived. At that time she handed me the allowance for January and February, because, according to her, the end was near and it was necessary to get in extra supplies of food as no one could tell what state of chaos would ensue.

To this day I am not sure which organisation Mrs Mariańska was working for. I know that she is living in Israel and, I suppose, it would not be too difficult to find this out from her.

My signature confirms that the above statement is correct. Genia Nussbaum.

I have deposited the above statement as told by the witness. Jona Leser.

Genia Nussbaum's report is so characteristic in certain details, which are capable, better than any description, of clarifying the problems connected with the fate of Jews in hiding as well as with our work in the Council, that we are quoting it here almost in its entirety. At the same time it is necessary to correct one fragment. I really do not know where Mr Niewiara got the information that I used to ride around Kraków in a horse-drawn cart selling vegetables. It is true that on at least two occasions, while working in the Bronowice garden, I took, that is I helped to deliver, some fruit and vegetables to the German store and this was simply within the framework of the quota imposed by

NEW CONTACTS - NEW METHODS

the Germans. It could well be that Niewiara happened to meet me in the street when I was involved in this. The other possibility which comes to mind, could be my visits to his house while I was carrying a rucksack full of vegetables for my own use. All this proves how certain legends come into existence. This information about the vegetable cart in which money and documents, and even clothes (which I never distributed, as funds for this purpose were available), were hidden, is repeated, after Genia Nussbaum's account, in Efraim Dekel's book *Saved from Extinction*, published in Tel-Aviv in 1963.

But this is not the most important thing in this story. The simple fact that an accident of fate and sheer coincidence saved these women, proves in what strange ways human fortunes crossed one another during those inhuman times. What would the fate of these three women and one child have been, if they had remained without any means of paying for their hiding place, at that time, during the last months of the war, and if they had been forced one day on to the streets, after more than a year living without daylight and fresh air? Where could they have gone? Where would they have searched for another hiding place, without money and without documents and with an appearance which gave away their origin at the first glance? We did see a lot of these people from the shelters, both during the occupation and after the war: these were cavemen of the new era, the era of Nazism.

Genia Nussbaum and my paths crossed in the one place to which I had been drawn by instinct, she by hope. Today I think about what role Niewiara played in this; was it only a passive one? Could it be that he, a Polish socialist, played the main role after all - as both Genia and I are writing about it independently? This is a topical question, as it has relevance to the campaign to award honours to the *Hasidei Umot Haolam* or the 'Just among the Nations'. As I participate in the meetings of the commission which awards these honours, I am constantly witnessing discussions on the subject whether or not the person in question had endangered his own life when he extended any sort of help to the persecuted and hounded Jews. With all due respect to my colleagues, I must admit that I am not always successful in convincing them where this type of campaign is involved. It is true that Niewiara did not hide Genia, but is it not a fact that this Jewish girl, by her own admission with a strikingly semitic appearance, was coming to his house and could very well have been followed by an informer or Gestapo agent, and therefore carried a threat to him and his family? At the present time this is a rhetorical question, but in those days it had an entirely different meaning.

9

PARTING

MORDECAI

It would be difficult for us not to include in these memoirs the days and nights of our everyday life, the hours which passed between one action and another. Action, not in the sense of the Holocaust, but on the contrary, the action of co-operating with an aid and rescue organisation or incidents where we were able to provide individual help. Our personal life was comparatively impoverished in comparison with our secret activities. But it also made normal human demands on us. We had to eat, find something to wear, find accommodation and simply to live and live among people. But there were different sorts of people around. First of all, everyone was divided into those who either knew or had been initiated into our 'Aryan' status, and the others, in relation to whom one had to pretend to be, like themselves, indifferent to the tragedy which was taking place in front of our eyes. This life was a stage, on which we were actors. We played our role well. But it is hard to convey how much stress there was and how much will-power was required, not to lose one's self-control because of the feeling of outrage, the heart-rending pain in the face of the wickedness and villainy, not necessarily of anti-Jewish activity, but sometimes only in words and expressions. Silence and clenched teeth; the situation dictated it. After all the years of freedom, this is still reflected in the nightmares, the unwritten and unspoken chronicle of memories.

And next to these 'local' experiences, there was the thought about the rest of the world, about the silence of this world, about the hypocritical attempts at compassion, about the immense distance, not only in space, between that which was happening here in front of our eyes, and the ideas of those people from the free world.

I try hard to recollect what role the events of the war played in our everyday experience. After all, we did soak up the news from secret broadcasts and we searched it out in the underground press. By 1943 it was possible to find out about the 'readjustment of the front' in the East in Soviet Russia even from the German-inspired gutter press. In February 1943 came the German defeat at Stalingrad, and in March the liquidation of the Kraków ghetto, German setbacks on the African front and at the same time Jewish setbacks 'on all fronts'. During the same period when hopes that a German defeat was close at hand were growing, when the German–Italian axis had been broken, I witnessed the Jewish calamity in the Janowski Camp. The heroic burst of the Warsaw ghetto fighters left behind it the amazement and admiration of the so-called world – as well as the smouldering ruins, the ashes, thousands of corpses and thousands of people sent to their death. This was the state of our hopes. We watched as our Jewish calamity was being perpetuated along with the inevitable progress of Hitler's defeat.

During this period I thought a lot about my family, over there beyond the ocean. At that time I had three sisters and a brother in Argentina and Brazil. What did they know about us? What sort of news was reaching them and did they believe it? To this day I find it difficult to talk to them about this subject. It is quite certain that they were not indifferent to our fate, but they were in the grip of the same helplessness and impotence which characterised the whole distant world in its attitude to the Jewish tragedy.

Several years after the war I read Albert Camus's novel *The Plague*. I do not know if the author was using an allegory, I only know that I got the following impression while reading it: here is a description of a terrain which has been cut off from the rest of the world and has been infected with the Nazi plague. One chapter, in particular, seemed to me to have been taken from this gloomy reality, our reality. They are the thoughts of the doctor who has remained in the plague town.

> Sometimes at midnight, in the deep silence of the empty town, when the doctor got into his bed in order to sleep

PARTING

his all-too-short sleep, he would turn the radio dial. From all corners of the world, unknown fraternal voices, many thousand miles away, clumsily attempted to express their solidarity and they really did express it, at the same time exhibiting a terrible impotence, which befalls every human being when he really wants to share the suffering which he cannot see: 'Oran! Oran!' This call traversed the seas in vain, in vain Rieux waited in readiness; the eloquent words further deepened the fundamental difference which emphasised the fact Oran and the speaker were strangers to each other. 'Oran! Yes. Oran!' But no, the doctor thought, to love or to die together, there is no other way out. They are too far away.

This was our truth – 'they' were too far away. And this justifies them in their own eyes.

The year 1943 was a difficult one. Hopes melted like lumps of snow under the gloomy and sunless sky of the spring, summer and autumn. We were struck a heavy blow, as in the summer of that year our infallible friend and director, Zygmunt Kłopotowski was arrested. In spite of this I did not give up my work. My trips to Lwów continued up to the liquidation of the Janowski Camp. I went everywhere in the service of the Council for Jewish Aid, referred by 'Teodor'. I no longer remember the names of all the people to whom I brought documents and money. But I missed Kłopotowski very much, his wise council, his good will and endurance in his activities for the benefit of persecuted people. During the last period of my activity in the Lwów area, when Borwicz was already 'free', there was a lot to do in order to find some sort of arrangement for little Janka Hescheles. Miriam and I were very much involved in these affairs. In autumn of the same year, there was another disaster: Ziutka Rysińska, our brave contact, was arrested. It seemed as if death, which had till then hovered in the distance, was circling around us, closer, ever closer.

In December a decision which was initiated by 'Teodor' was made, that I should escape to Hungary. I will not attempt to describe my feelings at the thought of parting from Miriam after four years of working together. Such matters are too personal. However, she had a positive attitude to this project. There was good news reaching us from Hungary. Many Jews with Polish names managed to sneak across the border. It seemed as if, over there, one had a chance to live and to survive. I gave in largely due to a state of mental exhaustion. But this was not the only reason. I must admit that there was an element of curiosity, a desire for a new adventure, a need for a change, an opportunity to tempt fate and to try one's powers in a new territory in it as well. In January 1944 I found myself, along with several other passengers and a guide, in a small railway station near Kraków. Miriam and 'Teodor' saw me off. My leather jacket was not to 'Teodor's' taste, and he said that it attracted attention and made one stand out among the normal travellers. Without further ado, he took off his black cloth jacket and we swapped garments.

My trip to Hungary and my sojourn in that country up to the end of the war and for several months afterwards, form the subject of a separate story, to which I shall return. I witnessed the bombing of Budapest, I was with the Soviet Army when Vienna was taken, but these fragments form a different part of my experiences. I will leave all this for later. Meanwhile I am travelling in a train: while setting off into the unknown, I did not suspect that in less than two months I would again find myself under German occupation.

MIRIAM

A new era in my life began at the start of 1944. I was alone, but not lonely. It was only thanks to my work, which was intensive, full of emotional involvement and continuous stress, that I was able to surmount this crisis. My life companion and co-worker left me, the one who had been able, in times of difficulty and total collapse, to defuse the situation and to strengthen my confidence in my own capabilities with his own courage and his unshakable self-assurance and optimism.

The very first news we had from Mordecai from Hungary did not reach us until the summer of 1944 at Jadwiga Kruczkowska's house. Two or three postcards to him and from him have survived. By that time it was already known that the Germans had taken over Hungary, which up till now was thought to be safe. The movement of Jews across the border had ceased.

The good omens were the German defeats on all fronts, but

PARTING

above all the opening of the second front in the West. But how very distant liberation appeared for all those whose battlefield was not in Russia, Normandy or Africa, but here, in the camps, in the bunkers and in the state of continuous danger of living on Aryan papers.

In June of that year we lost Adam Rysiewicz ('Teodor') from our ranks. He died in Ryczów in the station on the border which divided the General Government from the German Reich, while returning from a meeting with his Auschwitz contacts. At that time a plan for Cyrankiewicz's escape from Auschwitz was being worked out. It is difficult to dwell upon this loss, after all, I had experienced many losses before then, but this blow was particularly painful and it aimed at the heart of the underground organisation and at the hearts of all of us who had known and loved him.

In the summer of 1944, for the very first time since I lost my family and the only solace I could find was in my work, my thoughts about life under this cursed occupation took on a different dimension. In spite of everything, it became worthwhile to survive until such time as one would see the Germans retreat. The city, which had become Germanised to such an extent that the German tongue could be heard all over the streets, was now blocked up with suitcases, chests and all sorts of baggage containing stolen property which the German families were trying to send back to their crumbling fatherland. But this spectacle was not the one that gave me the most pleasure. From time to time I would still walk along the Bronowice road to work in the garden, as I continued to need that contact, and sometimes I had to sleep several nights there when something suspicious was going on in Kraków. Along this very same road, on certain days, one could see the German Army running headlong away from the East. And it was not an Army in the sense of some sort of organised military power, but rather Army men using all sorts of vehicles, mostly motorcycles. The year 1939 came to mind, the same soldiers and officers, spotless, clean-shaven and scrubbed, wearing brand-new uniforms, with flashing smiles and throwing sweets to Polish children, conquerors who were going to overrun the world. Now they resembled the Jews who were being driven to the camps: there was fear in their eyes, they were unshaven and dirty, and they were hurrying as if the Russians were already breathing down their necks. Later on, when the front stabilised somewhere near Rzeszów, this flood of refugees stopped and it was not until January 1945 that I lived through the unforgettable experience of the liberation of Kraków.

10

JANKA'S WANDERINGS – WANDA AND JADWIGA

MIRIAM

Even though neither Mordecai nor I remember the exact date of the following events, it could well have been a short time before I started in the Council for Jewish Aid, after Kłopotowski's arrest; we were receiving ID cards for Jews from 'Teodor' and from Wójcik. This continued until one day, Władek Wójcik handed me a parcel followed by a short commentary, as follows, 'Our legalisation office has burned down, so try and find some place where you can paste in the photographs and stamp the documents. You will find a pattern in there. Someone else will fill them out by hand.'

He gave me the address where I must immediately, and he emphasised the word 'immediately', deliver the stamped ID cards. Our meeting took place in the street. In my hand I had a load, not a very large one, but no less dangerous than a revolver or grenade; it was a packet of blank ID cards and stamps, including a round one saying, GENERAL GOUVERNEMENT DER STADT – HAUPTMANN DER STADT KRAKAU with a crow and a swastika; an oblong one saying, DER STADTHAUPTMANN DER STADT KRAKAU, POLIZEIDIREKTOR (ABTEILUNG IIIC) IN AUFTRAG; and a third oval one, with the Kraków coat of arms and STADTVERWALTUNG KRAKAU – Municipal Government in Kraków. The latter was for registering at the appropriate address: there you are, it could not be more simple. Only to find a place, and very quickly too, as walking around town carrying such a load was not a very good idea. After thinking for a moment, I went to see Wanda.

WITNESSES

We met Wanda Janowska through her sister, Jadwiga Kruczkowska, Leon's wife. The Kruczkowskis had been friends of mine since before the war; Mordecai and I had something resembling a *pied-à-terre* in Jadwiga's place, who, to begin with, lived with her twelve-year-old son Adam on Dietla Street. It was always possible to drop in there for a minute or for a few hours if something nasty was happening in the nearby streets, such as roundups, unexpected searches, document checks or other pleasures of the occupation years, but sometimes simply for a rest, a talk and a glass of tea. Later Jadwiga moved to Wieliczka and my little Hania spent nearly a year there.

At that time Wanda was working as a beautician in a hairdresser's on Krakowska Street, and she lived with her mother in Podgórze. This work was only a pretence, just to be able to have some sort of certificate but Wanda also did cosmetic work at home, in order to earn some money, as she had no talent of any sort for trading, which was widespread among Polish women. We immediately became very fond of this beautiful, charming, helpful Wanda, and she has remained our dearest friend to this day.

So I headed straight for the beauty parlour. I briefly explained what it was all about and Wanda quite simply, without asking any questions, invited me to her house as if the matter concerned nothing more than some cosmetics. My 'load' was then placed on the small kitchen balcony, amongst other household rubbish. Mrs Janowska, Wanda's mother, knew only that something was going on behind her back. She probably guessed that that something was connected with secret work, but she did not interfere, neither at that time, nor later when they moved to a bigger flat on Wrzesińska Street, where our document factory was already working under full steam.

Wanda's flat was not really suitable for this kind of work, mainly because there was no room in it at all. It consisted of one room and a kitchen. It was in this room that Wanda used to receive her clients and acquaintances, and she always seemed to have a large number of both. It took some doing to be able to stamp ID cards and to paste in photographs at the same time as a client was settling down in the armchair, or a friend had dropped in. I used to storm into the place, in order to deliver an urgently needed ID card.

Wanda and I had an agreed sign system. This system worked

JANKA'S WANDERINGS - WANDA AND JADWIGA

perfectly, thanks to Wanda's imagination and unshakable self-confidence. She never showed any sign of nervousness, she was also totally devoid of any sense of reality, according to 'Teodor'. She was friendly, calm, balanced, and she liked to dress and eat well and also to flirt. This life style evoked total confidence to such an extent, that without any real basis I could not imagine that anything bad could ever happen to her.

The real measure of Wanda's untroubled faith in her own security was the fact that when she took on our 'workshop' in her flat, she did not even mention the existence of the Jew who, on his false document, was registered at her address and was hiding somewhere. The whole affair came to light much later on, at the same time as she took our charge, Janka Hescheles, a refugee from the Janowski Camp, into the same tiny flat. She was informed that the Jew had been arrested and she was to expect to be searched at any time. It then became necessary immediately to remove not only the document factory, but also Janka from the flat. At that stage Wójcik found another place which we used until Wanda moved to her new flat. For a short time I had to place Janka with my witch in the Little Market. From there she went on to the Kobyliński family, from where she also had to be urgently evacuated. But this is another chapter of the story entitled 'Janka's wanderings'.

The first and safest refuge for Janka was Wanda Janowska's flat in Podgórze. Both Mordecai and I made every effort to avoid putting Janka in hiding and to assure her at least a minimum of daylight existence. Janka wrote her own memoirs in that very same flat, and the notebooks filled with her childish handwriting followed quite different roads. Her memoir, entitled *Through the Eyes of a Twelve-year-old Girl* was published in 1946 by the Jewish Historical Commission in Kraków. I briefly described Janka's wanderings through many different flats in the introduction, but this description is far removed from the dramatic reality. This unusual document has also appeared in a German translation in East Germany, along with five other memoirs from the days of the occupation, under the title of *In Feuer vergangen*, with an introduction by Arnold Zweig (Berlin 1960). The historical value of this memoir is inestimable, as it was written in the heat of the moment, almost immediately after her escape from the Janowski Camp. We include two short fragments below.

> Daddy kissed me and said, 'Janka, you are now 10 years old and you must become independent. Don't look at people you know and always be brave'. He kissed me again and wanted to say goodbye. I began to realise what was happening and I made out like I was going to cry, but Daddy said, 'If you love me, be brave and never cry, crying is humiliating both in happy as well as unhappy circumstances. Go home now and leave me alone.' I kissed Daddy for the last time and I went out.

This is how she said goodbye to her father, for ever. The next fragment concerns her stay in the camp.

> In Piaski, on the opposite side, the flames containing the burning corpses were belching. The air was filled with a poisonous stench. I missed Mummy, but I did not despair, I only envied the fact that it was all over for her. I am watching the flames in which she is probably burning and I know that I will also burn up in them.

Thanks to Ziutka Rysińska's efforts, Janka did find a place in the house of three women, a mother and two daughters, the Kobylińskis. I introduced her to them as being half-Jewish, a daughter of a Jewess and a Polish officer who was in England. This was another one of my lies told with the conviction that the end justifies the means. Janka spent quite a long time in this house, until one day she committed an error which presented new problems both for her and for us. She wrote a letter to Borwicz whom she knew from the camp and who had given Janka's name and the contacts which made her escape possible to the Kraków Council. In this letter she carelessly mentioned certain forbidden names. Before I could get hold of the letter, her protectresses had read it.

What followed has left behind a bitter taste – I had to explain my lie to these very sensitive ladies. And the final days of her stay there were also very hard for the girl. But it was not that which was the most serious problem. We had to look for another refuge for the not too careful Janka. She was not prepared to accept the numerous limitations of her 'freedom'. She had a habit of copying various fragments of her memoirs in the pages of a book she was reading. Some uninvited person would have been able to find and read this material at any time.

JANKA'S WANDERINGS – WANDA AND JADWIGA

She lived through her father's death immediately after the German entry into Lwów, as Henryk Hescheles, the editor, died in an Ukrainian pogrom along with Rabbi Lewin, when they were returning from an audience with Metropolita Szeptycki (the highest dignitary of the Eastern church) – and her mother's as well, who in fact, according to witnesses, poisoned herself along with several other members of staff in the hospital where she worked. She was not an easy charge. She did not know how, and did not really want, to adapt to the conditions of total secrecy. She continuously asked to be given a job in the underground and once she even went so far as to hide a bottle of petrol amongst her belongings, with a fantastic plan for some sort of anti-German action.

As an interim measure I again placed her with my landlady in the Little Market and both Mordecai and I searched for some way of saving her. But it was not until the autumn of 1944 that, by a stroke of great luck, I met Jadwiga Strzałecka at our treasurer's, Mrs Michalska's house, and the problem of Janka was solved in the best possible way.

This meeting was unforgettable. I had the privilege of meeting a human being of such unusual beauty and character, that to this day an image of this woman, her style and manner, and her unlimited commitment to the business of saving Jewish children has remained engraved in my memory. She was a director of a Warsaw orphanage and following the Polish uprising she and the children found themselves in Poronin. Among the forty children in this institution, there were ten Jewish children. When I told her about my problems connected with Janka, she immediate made the following suggestion, 'Please bring her here, and I hope that she will like it here among our children.'

This chance was a godsend. These final months of the war were, for Janka, a liberation from the nightmare experiences she had lived through. I visited the orphanage every month: I would bring along the Council's monetary allowance for Jewish children, but with the understanding that they could not really be treated in any special way. We left this question entirely up to the director. Considering the great risk she was taking on, she had a perfect right to use that money at her discretion. The institution's main official source of finance was the Polish Main Protection Council. It was not an easy undertaking to feed and clothe such a large group of children, and taking into consideration the fact that their numbers were constantly increasing, with those abandoned and orphaned after the Warsaw uprising.

During one of my visits I noticed a little girl with her head shaved and such strikingly semitic features, that astonished by the fact that she was going out for a walk with the other children, I asked, 'My dear Jadwiga, how can you bring yourself to send a child like this into the streets, after all, she can be recognised as Jewish at first glance.'

'That is exactly the reason why I cannot single her out from the rest', she answered briefly.

This was the principle she lived by. I never knew what her self-confidence was based on, but she radiated with something from within, a kind of gift from above which is the lot of a very few. In spite of the great social gulf between Jadwiga Strzałecka, the aristocrat, and Józef Jedynak, the miner from the Wieliczka salt mines, they nevertheless had something in common, namely, an indefinable mastery, a kind of prophetic quality. I have often thought, that in order to give a true picture of the character and activity of these two people, one would have to write a poem.

Among the staff in the orphanage in Poronin, there were also two Jewish women, Dr Heller, a qualified doctor working there as a nurse; the other one was a tutor. It was there that Janka survived during the final months of the war. She writes about it in a letter to Marek Arczyński in connection with the publication of the work entitled 'The Cryptonym "Żegota" '.[1]

> From the very first moment when I crossed the threshold of the house in Poronin and met its director, Jadwiga Strzałecka, the status of a young girl was returned to me. I was again surrounded by kindness, love and care. I would like to emphasise that all the children in that house were treated in the same way. There were more than fifty of us there. I was put in a room together with some slightly younger than me. These were the last months of the war. We had nothing more to do with it in our everyday

---

[1] M. Arczyński and W. Balcerak, 'The Cryptonym "Żegota", in the *History of Help to Jews in Poland 1939–1945*, 1st edn, Warsaw, 1979. The letter is included in the appendix, and the fragment quoted appears on p. 24.

existence. In the midst of beautiful mountain scenery, activities organised by our tutors, lessons and the friendliness which surrounded us, this orphanage was a fairy tale island. In those days no schools for Polish children existed. The tutors taught the younger children, and the older ones, and I among them, attended private lessons which were secretly held by a local teacher.

The last time I saw Jadwiga was in Paris in 1948. By then she was already very ill, but continuing to radiate her amazing, delicate beauty. She died soon afterwards. But she has remained as a treasure, untouched by time or experience in my memory and my heart.

11

THE REFUGEE FROM AUSCHWITZ

MIRIAM

Szymon Zajdów's story found its way into the fragments of my memoirs in Yad Vashem and was included in Israel Gutman's book *People and Ashes* (*Anashim ve Efer*, Kibutz Merchavia, 1957 in a Hebrew translation).

In the group of five escapees from the Auschwitz camp there were two Jews who were communists. One of them, called Meisel, was from Austria. He was smuggled out to the USSR. The other one who came from Warsaw, was referred to the Kraków Council for Jewish Aid by Teresa Lasocka, who used to receive Cyrankiewicz's reports from Auschwitz and looked after the refugees together with 'Teodor'. I am not able to give more precise details relating to these matters as we were not really directly involved with them and they had been strictly confidential. It was Władysław Wójcik who took Szymon over in Kraków, and it is from him that I found out this refugee's early history.[1]

---

[1] In 1980 in Frankfurt, a book in German appeared under the title *Nicht wie die Schafe zue Schlachtbank* (Not Like Sheep to the Slaughter). Hermann Langbein, the author, a former Auschwitz inmate and a member of an underground organisation which was active in the camp gives the following information about Zajdów (on p. 278):

> 'Józef Meisel, an Austrian Jew, who escaped from Auschwitz together with his Polish companion Szymon Zajdów, informs us that a Polish underground organisation in Kraków offered him help. Szymon, however, was left without any help whatsoever, as it was known that he was a Jew, a fact which was not known about Meisel.'

This information given by Langbein is based on a conversation with Meisel. As I was personally involved – and with me, my Polish colleagues from 'Żegota' – in helping Szymon Zajdów, I consider the above remark unjust with regard to the Polish–Jewish aid organisation in Kraków. Among the receipts signed by Jews who were receiving allowances, we also include in the appendix a copy of such a receipt signed by Zajdów himself.

THE REFUGEE FROM AUSCHWITZ

Because the matter concerned not just anybody – Zajdów had fought in Spain, and he was later taken out of an internment camp in France by the Germans and in Auschwitz he wore a red square, signifying that he was a political prisoner – his case was immediately taken up by socialist secret organisations. He was an extremely difficult charge, not only because of his appearance, but also due to his behaviour. His appearance was the quintessence of semitism. 'Baśka' – Hanka Kowalczyk – was the one who expressed it most emphatically in the following way, 'With this one you would not even have to let down his trousers to be sure!' And his behaviour was typical for people with a fighting background, who had managed to break out from camp or prison: they were under the illusion that they were really free. Quite simply they were not afraid enough.

Szymon, for whom a place in Kraków, in a good flat which was empty all day long, was found at the beginning, started to get bored. He would approach the window, despite the fact that this was strictly forbidden, and in the end he managed to chat up some girl in the flat opposite. One lovely day when he had enough of loneliness, he obeyed her call and went to her. Naturally I do not know the precise details of this flirtation, but I do understand poor Szymon, who at this moment forgot all about his bad appearance and his other Jewish 'defects' – my goodness, after so many years of abstinence . . . . When the affair came to light, the owners of the flat demanded that he be removed immediately. So he was transferred into the custody of some trusted socialist activists somewhere near Wieliczka. They certainly must not have been too happy to harbour a communist, and one looking like him as well, but such were Party orders. I do not know what role women played at this stage, but the fact is that he did not stay there long either. It appears that he refused to remain in hiding and also got involved in fierce political discussions. It became necessary to change the place once more. Wójcik brought me a photograph and declared, 'An ID card has to be made and a place to live found for him immediately, which means tomorrow at the latest.'

With great difficulty I managed to beg two days' grace, but I had not the faintest idea where to turn to, as on top of everything else, Władek, in all honesty, said to me, 'Don't for a moment imagine that he really looks like on that photograph. You must be prepared for the fact that he can be recognised as a

Jew at first glance.' In the context of those times, this was not a very good reference.

It was just then that Ania O. got me out of this difficult situation. Without meeting the candidate at all, she found a place for him in a potter's house, where her sister and her little daughter were living. I must confess that in relation to these women, my conscience was not entirely clear, but there was no other solution to this problem. Originally, the landlord demanded two-and-a-half thousand złotys, but when he saw Szymon, he raised the price by a thousand. Just because of his nose! This was a horrendous sum, if one takes into account that in those days the charges received between five hundred to a thousand złotys a month, and it was known to happen that, if the money did not arrive on time, they might only get three hundred.

'Baśka' went to fetch Szymon from Wieliczka. She was a very brave girl, but in this instance she certainly was in a sweat. She told me afterwards that she would have preferred to smuggle a machine gun. She did however admit that Szymon behaved extremely well. He was so self-assured and calm, as if Germans had not existed at all and as if all Poles had been friendly to the Jews. 'Baśka' disguised him as an invalid by bandaging his entire face, including his nose, and told curious fellow passengers that she was taking him to hospital for an eye operation. I took Szymon over from her on Dietla Street. I did not consider such a bandage the safest thing, as it attracted the attention of passers by. We went into a gateway and I took off his dressing. Now it was my turn to break out into a sweat. I have no intention of hiding my true feelings at the time; in a word, I was terrified, as soon as his eyes, nose and head on which the short, curly, black hair was just beginning to grow back came into view. I decided to get to Dębniki by crossing the Wisła by boat. One was less likely to meet a policeman there, and people . . . well, people were everywhere. But in order to reach the river, one had to walk across the whole length of the Dietla Public Gardens. At first I wanted to tell Szymon to walk behind me, and in the event of something going wrong, to pretend that he did not know me, but I was overcome by shame at the thought of it. After all, this man was a soldier who had gone through the Spanish campaign and had faced up to the decision to escape from Auschwitz, which must have required more than a

THE REFUGEE FROM AUSCHWITZ

normal degree of determination considering his appearance, and he had behaved with great courage, without a trace of fear; so how could I show him that I was afraid? Well, it did turn out all right. In those days I learned to believe in simple human luck. And Szymon's case just shows that neither a good appearance nor the best papers mean as much as that mysterious ounce of luck.

So he stayed at the potter's house, but he would not, under any circumstances, allow himself to be bundled behind the wardrobe as the landlord wished. One day, two policemen, one Polish and one German, arrived at the flat. Usually Polish ones were more dangerous as they would have been much more aware of the significance of such a Jewish appearance as Szymon's. Ania's sister recounted the details of that adventure to me: they came upon Szymon as he was standing in the middle of the room with rolled up shirt sleeves and with a broom in his hand. As it happened, he had just made some paper cut-outs for little Tusia, and was getting ready to sweep up the scraps of paper. Who knows if it was not precisely this broom which saved his life; he looked so completely domesticated that they never even asked for his papers. They were looking for someone else, and asked if he was living in this house.

But another time the situation became much more dangerous. The Germans staged a raid on Dębniki as they were looking for a secret press. They, quite simply, went from house to house and from flat to flat. Our potter – without regard for the money which he was getting – told Szymon to leave the flat immediately. Szymon put on his jacket and his hat and went out as if he were going for a walk. He spent all day walking up and down the Wisła embankment, but no one stopped him, despite the fact that the place was swarming with police. Towards evening he was noticed by some sand diggers who were taking sand out of the river. They called him over, and asking no questions, put a spade in his hand and told him to get on with it. Szymon worked along with them until the evening, and by that time the raid was over. No one is ever likely to give a medal to these nameless individuals for this human gesture. And this was by no means the only such anonymous incident during our occupation experience.

But this was not the end of Szymon's problems, and mine

along with them. He wanted, at any cost, to join the partisans, and he could not sit still for the thought that one day he would be taken, in a helpless state, like a trapped rabbit. He demanded to be given a gun, but no one was prepared to do this for him. I did all I could to convince my colleagues that it really was senseless to keep this kind of man locked up. But the Polish Socialist Party had no partisan group to speak of anywhere in the vicinity of Kraków. Some fighting groups did exist, but there could be no question of letting Szymon join them. Finally, as a result of my very persistent requests, 'Teodor' brought me together with a representative of a communist cell in Kraków, a Professor Wyspianski, a well-known pre-war communist activist from Śląsk, as I was told. He was an old and very nice and honest man. I presented Szymon's request to him in very passionate terms, asking his help in assigning him to some partisan detachment. After all, this was a case of a man who not only had a high standing with the communists, but one with a fighting background as well. When we met for the third time, I was told that nothing could be done. I repeated this verdict to Szymon.

Just before the end of the war, he had to move once again, as the potter demanded it, and Ania once again came to my aid; this time she simply took him into her own family.

Right away, during the very first days of freedom, with a great sense of relief, I introduced Szymon to Professor Wyspianski who had just, if I am not mistaken, taken up the position of Inspector-General of Kraków. In any case this meeting took place at the first session of the City Council in liberated Kraków.

Szymon Zajdów, using the Polish name Kazimierz Wojnarek with which I christened him on his ID card, later became an important official: I think, but I do not remember all the details, a secretary of the Polish Workers' Party in the Pod Baranami building. We remained good friends in spite of the fact that he could not comprehend why I did not join the Party. In his opinion, a person without party affiliation is like a woman without sex appeal. But I think that he never counted on my becoming a party comrade of his and it may well be that he was glad that I remained a Jewish aid worker even after the war.

Despite our friendship we would frequently fall out, and once I remember being really indignant. This happened in the

THE REFUGEE FROM AUSCHWITZ

first post-war weeks, when Kraków looked like an international city because of all the foreigners who were passing through it. The city became a transit station for concentration camp survivors, mainly those from Auschwitz.

One day a delegation of Hungarian Jews appeared at the Committee headquarters. They were asking for help in transporting some invalids who had survived the march of death and were left behind in Auschwitz, but were not able to leave the camp on their own. I took them to see 'my' Szymon. If one wanted to get anything done, it was necessary to organise things, not through appropriate channels, which did not yet exist in any form, but through connections, referrals and nepotism. I considered Zajdów to be all-powerful, as far as contacts with the Russians were concerned, and it was only the Russians who would have been able to organise transport to Hungary. Szymon, sitting behind his desk, displaying his curly black hair which had grown back nicely and his Jewish nose which had caused us so much trouble, asked in a dignitary's tone of voice, 'But in what capacity are they here? As Jews or as communists?'

At this point I lost my temper: 'They have come as people', I said angrily, 'whose surviving relatives are still in the camp, helpless and sick, because the new regime cannot find the time to take care of such details. Perhaps you can remember that when you were in hiding, no one was asking you whether you were only a Jew or only a communist! For Władek, for 'Baśka', for Countess Teresa, you were first and foremost a human being who needed help . . .'

He did not let me finish. 'You were always a hothead!' he said. 'It's amazing that you managed to survive.'

And he took the Hungarian delegation to see the Soviet Army command. And even then they had to wait four weeks before this transport was finally organised. But this fact is not relevant to the present discourse. We intend to write about those postwar times at a later stage.

12

THE STORY OF A CELLAR

MIRIAM

I am not sure whether we realised how important all these documents and letters which we are publishing here for the first time would be when we describe our experiences. I never buried or gave anyone for safekeeping any of these precious papers, but always had them near me in very primitive hiding places and usually kept together with ID card blanks and other certificates destined for various charges. Nowadays all I have to do is to pick up one or the other of these letters, or simply some scrap, to be able to visualise human faces, as in a photograph, and to recall with absolute exactness the details of the stories associated with these people. It may well be that some minor episode has been lost to memory, but the basic things connected with my work in the Council for Jewish Aid in Kraków, have remained alive across the years.

In front of me I have the original letters which were written in the cellar on Ogrodowa Street in Mogilany. In the house of Adam Kowalski (pseudonym 'Konski'), who was a member of the Home Army, ten ghetto refugees had been hiding since March 1943. The first financial aid they received, came via the Home Army, specifically via 'Konrad' (it appears that one of the representatives of this organisation in Kraków used this pseudonym). One of the people hiding in the cellar, Lieberman, describes this contact in his declaration as follows.

> We heard that, and he [Kowalski] confirmed it, that the Home Army organisation also helps Jews. He was in contact with the chief distributor in Kraków and he told us that he will talk to him. [. . .] First he went and said that

THE STORY OF A CELLAR

he knows of a place where ten Jews are hiding. The other one replied, 'How is it that you come to us now, after a whole year has elapsed, when the Jewish question no longer worries us?' And he said, 'I know but these are my friends.' He was not prepared to say that we were staying with him. He only came to ask us to write a letter that we are requesting help and that there are ten of us, and we all had to sign it. We said that it was all right [. . . .] The next day he came and said: 'Chaps, help is coming' [. . . .] And it turned out that a few days later he brought us 10 thousand złotys, a thousand per person. This helped us tremendously. It was enough to buy food, but we had nothing to wear. The next month he also brought us 10 thousand, and we thought that this was manna from heaven and that we would somehow survive the war. However, all this ended after two months, as then the Polish uprising in Warsaw broke out and the contact with us was broken.

This contact was renewed thanks to Hanusia, who had worked in the Lieberman household before the war, and was now hiding Ania and her family. In October 1944 we received the first letter from this group. I quote below fragments of this and some of the following letters.

F.A.O. The Jewish Committee Kraków 12 X 1944
Many thanks for the help you have so far extended to us. Because of raging price rises and the approaching winter we are sending you the following request.
Since 13.3.1943, i.e. since the day of the liquidation of the Kraków ghetto, from which we managed to escape via the sewers at the last moment, we find ourselves homeless outcasts. We have been surviving till now from the few things we had managed to salvage, so that now all we have left is a few rags. We ask you to contact us directly, if this is at all possible, so we can describe our critical situation to you. The support which we are receiving at the moment makes it possible to survive in our present situation, but it is inadequate, despite our very modest expenditures. In addition one of us is supporting a six-year-old daughter, for whom he is forced to pay 1,200

złotys a month, and his part of the allowance amounts to only 1,100 złotys.

Therefore, in order to be able to better describe our situation to you, we again ask you to contact us. This contact is possible in Mr Konski's flat, who has rendered us many services and it is because of his intervention that we are now receiving support.

We wish to express the hope that your response to our request will be positive and that you will send us a prompt reply, for which we would like to thank you in advance and we remain forever grateful.

On the reverse, our treasurer, Mrs Anna Dobrowolska ('Michalska') had written in pencil, 'Ask them to say what items of clothing they need.'

In the next letter handed to the Council by a Polish woman friend of one of the people in hiding, who also gave them material help for as long as she was able to (I do not know her name), there was no longer any question of a face-to-face meeting. This was as a result of Kowalski's moods, who quite suddenly withdrew his permission. Lieberman's description sheds further light on this man's character: brave to the point of madness, not afraid of anything or anyone, but at the same time he would frequently lose his temper and would drive 'his' Jews to despair.

In a letter dated 8 December 1944 Lieberman writes

> As far as a face-to-face meeting with representatives of the organisation is concerned, the situation looks like this: for a long time now none of us have been leaving our hiding place, so as not to put ourselves at risk, and not to endanger others who are risking their lives for our sake. We therefore ask you to deal with any matters concerning us, through our friend and intermediary.

When the Council met, however, it was decided that someone must go and investigate the situation in person. Such large amounts of money were involved that any further allowances required supervision. I agreed to go and visit the group in hiding. It appears that Kowalski was not able to oppose this plan, because only two days after receiving the last letter, the

THE STORY OF A CELLAR

contact took me to Ogrodowa Street in Mogilany. Lieberman describes this meeting as follows

> Mrs Mariańska came to the meeting. This meeting took place on 10 December 1944. We talked for quite a long time and she promised us a lot of good help, that we would get everything we needed and that we should not worry, as we would get some clothes. They sent us 10 thousand złotys for the month of December and at the end of December or beginning of January we received a further 25 thousand złotys for clothes and winter stocks. We bought some fat, potatoes, cabbage and coal and we hoped that things would work out somehow.

For me, this experience was unforgettable. Only two of the men came out of hiding into Kowalski's flat, who, by the way, was present throughout the meeting. These two were wearing trousers and slippers made from paper sacks and their sunken, pale faces bore witness to the conditions in which they were living, without daylight and without fresh air.

From Lieberman's description it follows that their will to survive and their resourcefulness in organising their daily life, made it possible for them not to succumb to despair even during the hardest times. The fact that Kowalski put a radio down in their cellar played an enormous part. He said, and rightly so, that if the Germans should find ten Jews hiding in his flat, then their fate, along with his own, would be exactly the same, with or without a radio. And for these people, voices from the rest of the world, whether they fully understood them or not, were like a breath of freedom. They also used to listen to the Polish language broadcast from London, which lasted a few minutes every night at six p.m. They would also keep in mind a talk which had been given by a Rabbi in which he had said, 'I cannot help you, let God help you . . .' It was from these broadcasts that they learned that the Soviet offensive had finally begun. They sent word to me, through their contact, to buy in stocks of food, as Kraków might be under a lengthy siege and there might be nothing to eat!

One more episode from Lieberman's story, filled with dramatic incidents, should be recounted here. The Kowalski's cellar bordered on the cellar of their neighbour, who was a postman. When the postman realised that Jews were in hiding there, he deliberately picked a quarrel with Kowalski and broke off all relations. After the war he explained to the survivors why he had done so. Once again I give the floor to Lieberman,

> He forbade his wife to go and see her neighbour and this was supposedly because they had fallen out . . . . He told us that he did not want to get in our way and did not want to end up being an informer. He had nothing against the fact that there were Jews hiding there, but he had to take his household, his wife and children, into consideration. He said, 'If the Gestapo comes, I can say that I am not on talking terms with my neighbour, I don't want to know him, and we fell out a long time ago.' And this is how this neighbour lived next door to us for two years. When we used to listen to the radio at six o'clock, we found out later that he used to come, bringing a plate with him, which he would hold against the wall, and in this way he was able to hear as clearly as we could in our cellar. When we went out into the street, he would, while coming home drunk, say, 'Mr Kowalski, there is no radio, there are no broadcasts, we don't know what is going on', it was then that we knew that he was aware of our presence there.

Our contact with this group of survivors did not stop at the end of the war. In liberated Kraków these people, who had barely managed to shake off the dramatic experiences they had lived through, set to work energetically. They found a large ex-German or, rather, ex-Jewish flat on Starowiślna Street, at the corner of Dietla Street, for themselves, and as proof of their gratitude and friendship suggested that I move in with them. They set aside one room for me. I took advantage of this hospitality without much reflection. From their point of view this was a gesture of open-heartedness, but from mine, of foolhardiness. For at that time all survivors were looking for somewhere to live, but I remained a subtenant for a very long time until my Mordecai came back from Hungary. Afterwards, with the greatest difficulty, we managed to get a tiny, one-room flat, where we nested along with our son, born in 1946, until our departure from Poland in December 1948. It was during this period, almost immediately after the liberation of Kraków, that the Jewish Committee came into being. Before I had a chance to take any decisions in my personal life, Salo

THE STORY OF A CELLAR

Fischgrund arrived from Warsaw, and shortly afterwards Arie Bauminger from Lublin, and I settled down, in a manner of speaking; on the one hand there was the Committee and looking after the child, and on the other, my collaboration with the Jewish Historical Commission. So I really had very little time left to look for somewhere to live. But this does not form part of this chapter of our memoirs.

13

CONTACTS WITH WARSAW

MIRIAM

I went to Warsaw many times during the second half of 1942 and the beginning of 1943, before our own legalisation office was activated. Warsaw ID cards could be obtained by contacting Bronisława Langrod, who at that time lived in Warsaw. I have no information about her connections and I do not know from which organisation she used to obtain these documents, I only know that they had to be paid for. Ziutka Rysińska had a group of Jews in Debiça for whom she used to handle many different matters, among these was the supply of ID cards. She would bring photographs and money, and as not all of them had funds available for this purpose, she would make every effort to supply these people with documents using some of the money belonging to others. Enough money had to remain to pay for my journeys, as I was not able to pay for these 'outings' out of our own material resources.

My own trips, as well as Mordecai's, to Lwów passed without serious incident, but it must not be imagined that they all were completed without many interesting adventures. I found various ways of avoiding dangerous situations. For example, I became convinced that during sudden document checks, when, for example, all the carriages would be evacuated in one of the stations and selections were made outside, women with small children would be likely to go free. In such cases I would take advantage of the first available chance and would borrow a child from a mother who was lucky enough to be armed with two. I did not allow the woman any time to think, and would only say quickly, 'I will help you', and I would take the child by the hand or, which was even more reliable, on my arm. Children are children, and they were sometimes so frightened and stunned that they did not even protest, and even if they did cry and tried to escape, then, as it happens, this behaviour did not make the Germans suspicious. Usually, there was such a crush and confusion, that all they did was roar furiously, 'Zuruck! Zuruck!', and they would drive the women with children back into the carriages. That was all I really wanted. I would then find time to explain everything afterwards, and I always met with understanding. Naturally not as a Jewess, but as a young woman who was trying to avoid being deported for forced labour. All this confirmed the bitter truth, namely that a Polish child meant salvation to a Polish woman, but for a Jewish one it was her undoing. How many young, healthy mothers went to their deaths when attempts were made to pull their children out of their arms during selections in the camps?

The searches for smuggling were quite different. In those days hundreds of Poles, mainly women, travelled to Warsaw with all sorts of foodstuffs. They supplied everything to the capital, butter, bacon, sausage and eggs, not excluding moonshine. Moreover, they frequently ended up in camp or prison as a result. I had tremendous respect for these people, brave, shrewd and simply nice. In the end their activity became a form of resistance against German constraints. They were very well organised and had reliable information about certain specially dangerous stations. When the police would burst into the first carriage, they warned one another. In such cases they would try to hide anything possible anywhere they could. Sometimes the toilets in the trains were completely piled up with food. This was not very appetising, but it made it sometimes possible to save at least a part of the goods. The main thing was that the consumers knew nothing about it. Sometimes the incidents had a funny side. Once, a boy, who had been sent by the smugglers, burst into my compartment, 'The blue ones! They are taking everything.'

At this point it should be mentioned, and certainly not to the glory of the Polish police, that people were more afraid of the blue ones than of the Germans. The smugglers insisted that you could sometimes talk your way round the Germans, but in general the men in navy-blue were without mercy. It could be that they lived in fear of their German superiors.

A buxom peasant woman was sitting in the compartment.

She was holding a large round basket on her lap. The wonderful aroma of smoked sausage awakened a healthy appetite in every one of us. We made jokes about it. When she heard that the men in navy-blue were taking everything, the woman opened her basket, broke up the sausage rings into generous portions and handed everyone a piece of the sausage: 'Enjoy it. If they are going to take it away, at least let people eat it.'

It was a worthwhile experience to see the faces of the two policemen when they burst into the compartment. With an innocent expression on her face, the woman pointed at her basket and said, 'You want some? There's a piece left!'

In the Warsaw railway station I witnessed the following scene: a peasant woman watching the carnage which was being perpetrated by the police among the smugglers, slammed her basket full of eggs against the ground. 'Let them guzzle up these scrambled eggs!' she shouted and quickly disappeared into the crowd.

It is hard to explain how, in the face of a tragedy like the one we were witnessing, involved in work which was tied up with the fates of so many hounded and persecuted beings and the tension of one's own experiences, what effect such small, insignificant incidents had on us. They signified a breathing space, moments of escape from the bitter reality.

Sometimes the smugglers would ask me, when they noticed that my luggage consisted of nothing more than one small suitcase, 'Is this all you are carrying? Maybe you will say that you bought this goose. For I have got two of them and they are bound to take one of them away . . .'

'Why not? ' I readily agreed to such a deception. 'This is my goose, a present for my family', I would say to the policeman. 'This is a kilogram of butter for my sister in Warsaw, I am not going to sell it.' And in my small suitcase I had photographs and cards containing details necessary for making ID cards.

But I also had my secret hiding places. I would, for example, take with me some colourful children's toy like a jigsaw puzzle in a cardboard box. These boxes looked innocent, but they had false bottoms. But they were never searched, so I cannot say whether or not they would have stood the test. There was no test.

In spite of the fact that the streets of Warsaw were swarming with many informers, collaborators and stool-pigeons, both

CONTACTS WITH WARSAW

Polish and Jewish ones, the city always awakened in me feelings of admiration with regard to its general attitude to the occupiers. At every visit I would come upon a poster somewhere, in front of which people would stop for a moment and then would quickly disappear after having read it. These were short, but pithy protests against police actions, information about the latest show street-executions, promises of retaliation and threats directed at the murderers. In the places where the victims' blood had barely dried, heaps of flowers would appear and candles would burn. The red German posters which I knew from Kraków, announced that the following hostages had been condemned to death for the killing of a German policeman or some other German dogcatcher, and the names of the condemned would be given. People would stop and read, with faces congealed with fear and horror, seeking their dear ones among the names. They said nothing, and only the expression in their eyes spoke for them.

There were also other posters, both in Warsaw and in Kraków, saying things like 'Jew – lice – spotted typhus', with an appropriate illustration and other ignominious slogans. One did not have to keep silent at the sight of such posters, and the expressions which I sometimes heard, which I do not wish to repeat, would plunge anyone into a state of despair. And that meant every thinking person, not only a Jew, who happened to be passing by. I did see a large number of Poles who were offended to the depth of their beings by this vile propaganda, at least the Poles with whom we were working. But how many were there like them? Who is able to estimate their numbers?

I remember an incident connected with the never-to-be-forgotten Adam Rysiewicz. I accidentally bumped into him on a tram. I pretended not to know him in compliance with his strict orders, thinking to myself: if he himself pretends not to recognise me, I must obey it. So I stood next to him, looking the other way. Then a young boy appeared in the tram and he was singing a vile little song, a product of occupation 'creativity'. It went something like this: 'In the Saski Gardens, around the fountain, there are no more nice Jewish maidens . . .' and so on. I do not recall the rest of the words, full of poison and delight at the purged state of the Saski Gardens. People were dropping money into his hat, but not all, some of them turned their backs. It could be that among them were not only those who

151

begrudged him the pennies, but also those who were ashamed of this Polish song. I looked at 'Teodor'. I saw him clench his teeth so hard that his jaw turned white. At the next stop he took the young singer by the collar and threw him out of the carriage, but carefully so as not to hurt him. He himself remained inside. I was afraid of what the passengers' reaction was going to be, but no one said a word. It was an unimportant incident and it did nothing to help heal the wounds, but it soothed the pain somewhat.

When I started working in the Council for Jewish Aid, I went to Warsaw several times to meet the members of the Headquarters. It was then that I met Dr Berman, Leon Feiner ('Mikołaj'), Szymon Gotesman ('Józef Bogucki') and Salo Fischgrund. I already knew Marek Arczynski from the Kraków meetings in which he very often took part. I do not remember the exact dates of these meetings, with the exception of one of them, which has especially stuck in my memory. It took place in a flat on Żurawia Street at the beginning of November, it may even have been on the first of November, 1943. This time I came together with Władysław Wójcik. In his capacity as secretary of the Kraków Council, he reported on our activities: mainly he reported details concerning our charges in the city and its surroundings and in the Płaszów camp. I remember this particular meeting because of a specific incident, namely, Dr Berman announced the news that this same day or perhaps on the previous day, one of the chief Jewish stool-pigeons, Lolek Skosowski, had been liquidated.

Part of our correspondence with Headquarters has been preserved in our private archive. It consists mainly of my letters to Dr Berman dating back to different periods of our collaboration. Most of them were written after the Warsaw uprising, when the Kraków Council was looking after Warsaw refugees. We also have some of Szymon Gotesman's writings, who was a Kraków advocate lawyer before the war and a member of the General Zionist Party. He survived the occupation in Warsaw, collaborating with the Jewish National Committee and the Warsaw 'Żegota'. It is easy to pick out, but much more difficult to decipher Leon Feiner's letters, which were written on small cards in tiny handwriting. A dramatic telegram from Stefan Grajek and Józef Sak can also be found among the documents, in which they write about the situation

CONTACTS WITH WARSAW

the Jews found themselves in after leaving Warsaw. A selection of this correspondence is included in the appendix. Wherever possible, we include explanations and comments illuminating the contents of these letters.

The Warsaw uprising scattered the banished population of the capital. In this mass of homeless people, deprived of all their possessions, there were also found Jews, who had until now tried to live on the 'Aryan side' in Warsaw, and who now had no documents, no roof over their heads and, for the most part, no money. Yet this situation had one positive side, although this may seem hard to believe. In this tragic situation, the situation of the Jews became equal to that of the Poles. Like the Poles, they had to apply for documents to the temporary offices providing aid to the refugees. They could give their former name and address, which could not be checked in the destroyed city, and, like others refugees, made use of the documents with which they were provided. Our Kraków office for creating documents began on a larger scale to produce such refugee papers with the right information. This did not continue for very long, since after an interval the German authorities began to control and pursue the refugees. There then began anew the production of *Kennkarten* from various places, with the exception now of Warsaw.

In Suchedniów, a small town near Kielce, three members of the Jewish underground found a hiding place after the uprising: Stefan Grajek, Józef Sak and 'Kazik' – Symcha Rathjazer – as well as the Pole, Marysia Sawicka, who had worked as a liaison officer and a young Jewish woman, Irena Gelblum. I received the instruction to visit this group. I brought them documents and money (50,000 złotys) which were given to me by Władysław Wójcik. I returned with a letter from Grajek,

Dear Mr Cz. ('Czerski' – Wójcik's pseudonym].
Thank you very much for the information contained in your letter. On the question of *Jus [Jüdische Unterstützung Stelle*], it will be most convenient to communicate orally at a convenient moment, as this is a very difficult problem. Yet in the present situation, there was no other way. I acknowledge the receipt of 50 zl. for which I thank you. We have made contact with a number of places, to which help will be sent immediately. The work camps which

were previously located in the Kielce area have been moved to Częstochowa. We will also try to reach there. If the action is to be properly undertaken, we need further sums of money. I am sure that you will try to find the necessary amounts. The best way would be to effect a transfer, if this can be done.

I am sure that I shall be in Kraków shortly and will then be able to discuss all matters with you personally.

With best wishes,
Stefan Gr.

Wójcik wrote a note on this letter, 'On 12 October 1944, Marianska handed Grajek 50,000z – 'Czerski'. The fact that this note does not observe the usual conspiratorial rules – the removal of three noughts and the change of the date – is important at the present time, as it often happens that I do not remember the exact date, and the amounts, which were described in fractions, are often misleading. Grajek's intention to come to Kraków came to nothing, as can be seen from one of his letters. Contact with Suchedniów was maintained until December 1944. Copies of letters included in the appendix give a picture of the activities of the Kraków Council and are a testimony of my part in it. What particularly strikes me to this day, is the official tone of these letters, the repeated thanks for money sent and business completed. But, after all, these were not favours, but the carrying out of duty, as far as it was possible. In our organisation we were not used to titles or formal modes of address and such 'heart-felt thanks'. But I only mention this in passing.

All the letters and requests were brought by Marysia Sawicka and Irena Gelblum. The contact with the Kraków Council had been made through Borwicz, who had had access to the Warsaw group even earlier on. The intervals between my trips to Suchedniów were never longer than the situation demanded, i.e. the acquisition or completion of documents or the necessity of carrying out some other urgent tasks, but the anxiety emitted from Grajek's letters was understandable, whenever they felt they were losing a newly achieved contact for even a week at a time.

During my last visit to Suchedniów, it was decided that 'Kazik' and Irena would come back to Kraków with me. In

Kielce the Germans stopped the train and completely evacuated all the passengers. This time I did not even make any attempt to try and find some woman with children; after all I had two Warsaw colleagues with me. They took us under convoy to a school yard and started checking everyone's documents. I had my work card and exemption from trench-digging work stamped on my ID card. Irena also had some sort of Warsaw certificate and they let both of us go. 'Kazik', however, was stopped. He was immediately taken behind an enclosure, where a group of young men was already gathered together, destination: deportation for hard labour. During this period the Germans were mobilising all possible work forces. They had even stopped sending Jews to the gas chambers.

This whole action was being carried out by rounders-up wearing uniforms of some sort of work organisation, but it was not the 'Organisation Todt' which we knew. I managed to pinpoint the leader of this action. He was a German, of advanced age, of reasonable appearance. Irena and I came back to the yard by a side gate and we launched our attack. He looked very tired and he was listening to my explanation with only one ear, but he did listen. I tried to appeal to his fatherly feelings: I told him about the young pair, just married, who had gone through the hell of the uprising and who are as innocent as children. Parting would constitute another tragedy for them. 'You probably have children yourself. Have pity on these young people and don't separate them after all that they have been through', I begged.

He immediately found an excellent, truly fatherly piece of assistance, namely, he would include Irena in the group, and let them be off to work together: That way they will be together: they are in no danger. In the meantime, 'Kazik' was making signs to us from behind the enclosure. We found out later that he was afraid that we, too, might get unnecessarily involved in conflict. But I did not give up. I continued to pester that German until he got fed up with me, and it could well be that I did manage to move him with all my chatter. He pointed 'Kazik' out to one of his group and we were all together again. But the tragi-comedy only began at this stage: the young couple decided that we ought to repay this nice German in some way. I do not know why I let them talk me into it. Instead of simply saying: 'Let this benefactor go to the devil', we found out where the

Germans were staying. We waited till the end of the action and I put 500 złotys into an envelope and Irena and I went to the hotel where they were living.

'Kazik' gives a slightly different version of this incident in his testimony deposited in Yad Vashem in 1961, namely that the German demanded a bottle of vodka or some other drink. But this is not what happened, and I remember this incident very clearly. In the hotel we found the Germans eating and drinking and they insisted on inviting us to join them and we barely managed to get out of that pleasure. I found our German and asked to speak to him for a moment. When he joined me in an empty room, I handed him the envelope. I wanted to go, but he held me back with one hand. With his other hand he opened the envelope and gave it back to me with indignation. I must confess that I felt very embarrassed when he said, 'For money? You think I did it for money? If I wanted to take money, it would not be such amounts. I could be very rich. If you want to repay me, give me your address in Kraków. I am an old man and I don't like hotels. If I am passing through Kraków, I would like a room in a private house, to rest and to eat a homemade meal.'

What an idea! To give him the address of the flat where the legalisation station was located. Without hesitation, I dictated an address to him, which was invented from beginning to end, a name and a street name and number. I am ashamed to admit it, that I felt a bit uncomfortable at the thought that this old man, who had done us a great favour, would be looking for this flat in vain, most likely calling me a *'verfluchte Polin '*. But I quickly forgot all about it.

In Kraków I found a room in the flat of a lonely lady in Osiedle Oficerskie for 'Kazik' and Irena and I looked after their affairs for some time longer. After that they managed for themselves.

Time was of the essence: one had to make documents for the Warsaw refugees, find places to live, and travel around to look after their affairs, all against time. One of such cases ended up in my hands through the intervention of my permanent client from Wieliczka, Fischgrund-Misiołek. It concerned Leopold Leinkram from Kraków, a member of the Bund. He and his wife had been living in Warsaw on Aryan papers and were involved in secret work. They were separated by the Warsaw uprising and Irena came to Kraków after many adventures, but

CONTACTS WITH WARSAW

Leopold, who was evacuated in an invalid transport, found himself in Wodzisław, a small town somewhere near Kielce. It was necessary to get him out of there. I was given the task of going to investigate. I was to find Wacław Wojnarowicz (this was Leinkram's Aryan surname) in the place where the Warsaw invalided refugees were kept, and to find out what his condition was, and if possible to transport him to Kraków. Where to and to what address were left to my own initiative.

I do not remember at which station I got off the train, as the train did not go to Wodzisław. I managed to get there by hiring a peasant cart. I was directed to the school which served as a temporary hospital. A hospital – my dear God – the patients were living in two large rooms on the floor which had been covered by straw. They were all eyes: could it be that someone was coming to see them, a relative or friend?

I was directed to Wojnarowicz. I saw a thin, dark unshaven man – a Jew. It was obvious to me at first glance. Luckily, everyone else in that room looked equally pathetic. But some of them were at least cleanshaven. He was lying in the corner under the window, which was very convenient, as I was able to whisper to him outside anyone else's hearing. I sat down next to him on the straw. I heard a story which proved to me once more that in those days no fantasy could match the reality. He had on him several hundred dollars, but not one penny in Polish złotys. He could not even afford to buy himself a glass of milk, as others were doing, and the food which was served to the patients was as one would expect under the circumstances. He could not pay the barber who came to shave the others. Quite simply, he was a living illustration of the story of a man in the desert, who is dying of hunger, with his pockets full of gold. He said that the doctor who had examined him knew that he was a Jew, and both of them were waiting impatiently till someone came to take him away. He was not certain how long he would be able to shield him from disaster, from some unexpected search.

The first thing I did was to take Leinkram's dollars away and, leaving him some money, I went to see the doctor. 'I have come to fetch Mr Wojnarowicz', I said.

I could see the relief in his face. We did not mention the subject of origin and he only said that he had a very serious lung ailment and he must be treated in a real hospital as quickly as possible. I asked him to somehow help me find some means of transport to Kraków. 'I can't transport him by cart and train in his present state.'

I only mentioned the problems of transport, but the doctor knew what I meant. He promised that he would try to send the patient in a German lorry, as he knew a soldier. He asked for the exact address. Without further thought, realising the urgency of the matter, I gave him 'Kazik's' address in Osiedle. But I had to have time to prepare 'Kazik' for this visit. We made arrangements for Wojnarowicz to come to Kraków the next day, and I went back to tell him this. My conscience was not entirely clear, but what can I say? There was nothing else I could do. To take him along with his dollars and his face would not just have been risky, but utter madness. I reassured him and said that everything will be all right and that in Kraków he would see his wife who is waiting for him and, in the meantime, I would be trying to find him a place in hospital.

I spoke to him of hope. A big word, which we used very rarely, but sometimes one had to resort to it as not everything could be built on even the most carefully worked out plans. And this is what happened this time. Later on I found out from Irena Leinkram that apparently the doctor's plan to bring the patient by lorry did not work out: they only took him as far as the railway station. He made his own way to Kraków and barely managed to drag himself to the address given. The fact that he was not caught on the way was nothing short of a miracle. In spite of all the disasters and horror of those days, more miracles used to happen than in the Old and New Testaments.

It was not possible for him to stay in the Osiedle flat for more than two or three days. During this time I mobilised our forces, that is Dr Helena Szlapak and the infallible Teresa Lasocka, and Teresa in her turn Dr Garbien, a friend who lived in Lwów. When he was told who it was, he found a place in a private clinic on Siemiradzka Street. It was very expensive, but there was no other way out. The money came from the organisation. It turned out that before leaving Warsaw, the Bund had distributed its funds amongst its members. I gave the dollars to Wójcik, and the money thus obtained paid for the clinic, the nurse and other items which were necessary for the care of the patient. This money lasted for a while, and not a very long one. I do not remember exactly, but it must not have been more than a few weeks.

After examining the patient Dr Garbien said that there was no hope. I was waiting in the hospital corridor when he came out and said that the first test carried out, namely the blood sedimentation rate, was appalling. This time no miracle happened. The man was dying, but he was dying in a clean bed, carefully nursed and in the presence of his wife. For a Jew even this was considered a luxury in those days, to die in such conditions. However cruel this may sound, it was necessary to make advance plans for a funeral, and for a normal, Christian funeral at that. One had to avoid suspicion at any cost. I had to undertake yet another duty, and that was to convince the patient to confess. Without confession, a funeral was out of the question. I tried to do this as gently as I knew how. When I first brought it up, Leinkram was indignant. He said that he thought I knew who he was, so how could I be trying to talk him into something which was contrary to his socialist ideals. I could not very well tell him that he was dying, so I found another way: I explained to him that in this clinic there existed a tradition whereby the priest came once a week to listen in turn to the confessions of every single patient. If he turned out to be the only one who refused to submit to this 'operation', suspicion would fall not only on him, but also on his wife and on me. This appealed to his good sense and he gave in. I imagine that these may seem to be minor matters, without significance in the eyes of a historian, but not for us; not for me and not for his wife who was sharing the last moments of life with the person dearest to her.

In Warsaw I managed to find, among others, Bela and Dziunek Treibicz, who came from my home town of Pilzno. Ziutka Rysińska had been in contact with them and it was from them that I got their address in Targówek, where they were living using false names. Dziunek was at that time a young boy of about eighteen and his sister a little older. Their experiences form a dramatic contribution to the complicated question which can be called 'Poles and Jews during the occupation'. They both had 'real' birth certificates, with the names of dead Poles. These they had bought during their temporary stay in Dębica. When the order about the duty of owning ID cards appeared in Warsaw, they decided to acquire legal documents. This was possible as they had the birth certificates and official registration documents. Bela's birth certificate carried the name of Helena Kuśnierz and the ID card was made out in that name. The most difficult moment for many Jews was having to appear in the office in person to collect the document. One had to be finger-printed and personally to place a signature under the photograph. It was precisely during such a moment of nervous tension that Bela signed her real name, Balbina Treibicz. This is how she herself describes this dramatic moment

> A Polish clerk who was sitting next to me waiting for my signature, looked at me and then at what I had written. For me, this instant felt as if I had signed my own death sentence. The girl whispered to me (her boss, the German commissioner, was sitting in the next room), 'What have you done?' Terror-stricken, I could not reply as I had a large lump in my throat. She however asked quickly: 'Do you have another identical photo with you?' I did have one, I gave it to her and she told me to wait in the corridor where other candidates were waiting their turn. I waited not knowing what I was waiting for, for salvation or for the Gestapo . . . . I don't know how long it took, but it seemed eternity to me . . . . She then called me again and in front of her was a new ID card, with all the required stamps and with the German commissioner's signature. She again whispered a warning, 'Do be careful . . .' I was very careful. I signed: Helena Kuśnierz, I made my fingerprint and I could not say anything more than 'thank you'. Thank you for saving my life. I will never know how this brave and noble Polish girl managed to explain to her boss the need to make another ID card, and I do not know her name. But she has remained a good spirit in my memory.

However, for the sake of objectivity, alongside this act of bravery and assistance, one of Bela's younger brother's experiences should be also recounted. The boy's face was excellent. He worked as a technician at Philips. Once, quite accidentally, he stumbled into two German policemen and a Polish civilian agent in the street. Suspected of being a Jew, he was taken to the police station and the infamous inspection was carried out. He was stripped. The Polish agent insisted, with absolute certainty, that the boy was a Jew. The policemen were not quite sure. They summoned, as the highest authority, a German police officer and he settled the argument; the boy was not a Jew. He even proceeded to explain in great detail, what this physical record of Jewishness looked like. The protest of the Polish expert had no effect and they let the boy go.

One more marginal comment about the fate of the Treibicz family follows. In Władysław Bartoszewski's work *This One is From My Country*, in the first 1966 edition, on pp. 278-9, the story of three women from the Treibicz family from Pilzno is included. The author of this story did not give her name, but only her initials, H. J., Kraków. The story contains about ten per cent truth, certainly not more. Bela and her brother are living in Israel, and in addition to them Henia's husband, Zygmunt Seifert from Bielsko who died in Israel also survived. The wife of the eldest brother Michał also remained alive: everyone else perished. There was no question of any deportation 'for labour in Germany', as the author of the passage claims. During the period of liquidation of the Pilzno Jewish population, a part of the family found itself under the protection of the owners of the Przybory Estate which was the property of Count Ref. For a time Prince Jabłonowski, the count's brother-in-law, helped them to hide. But in the end they met the same fate as all the other Pilzno residents, that is they were 'resettled' in Bełżec. Only the ones listed above remained alive.

Rectifying facts in reports from the time of the Holocaust, which have been published in many different places, is not easy and cannot always be successfully achieved. However, when the facts are clear, as is the case here, it has to be done. This is the way I understand my own duty in such situations.

14

FOR WHOM THE BELLS OF VICTORY TOLLED

MIRIAM

Following the advice of my charges, the Liebermans, on 19 January 1945 I went to the Kraków market place in Wolnica, in order to stock up on food. The Russians were approaching Kraków. The Germans had made the city ready for a siege. The entrance gateways to all the houses along the main streets had been bricked halfway up and anti-tank trenches all around Kraków were being dug throughout several months in 1944; everything pointed to the fact that Kraków was going to be defended.

So there I was in Wolnica, when suddenly three Polish tradeswomen in a state of panic burst in with the following incredible news: they had gone to Słomniki to buy bacon, and they had seen three Soviet tanks. These had driven into the town and had gone out again immediately, but there was no doubt about it, they had been there, with the insignia of the Soviet Army and soldiers wearing white sheepskins and fur hats. The women swore by everything that is holy that they had seen all this with their own eyes, but no one in the crowd, which had gathered around them, would believe them. How could this be, after all Słomniki was to the north of Kraków, so how could the Russians be possibly coming from there?

But this is how it really happened. Kraków was taken as if by the Soviet sickle; it was surrounded and cut off from the west. Shopping was now out of the question, I felt, I knew that the thing that was happening was indeed the very moment which everyone knew must come for a long time now; but at the time my heart was bursting at the thought that it was happening at

FOR WHOM THE BELLS OF VICTORY TOLLED

last, that it had come, that it was coming nearer and nearer, that it had finally arrived. In the same way as in 1944, when the first German retreat began, I thought that it had been well worth living through it all. To survive and to be able to see Germans caught in a mousetrap in the streets of Kraków. And they really did look like rats caught in a trap. On Wielopole Street there was a long line of German tanks facing west. Around them soldiers and officers were milling round and it was clear that they had no idea which way to go. Shooting could be heard and shells were criss-crossing the streets and heavy smoke was billowing upwards from fires in the vicinity of the railway station. The Germans had set fire to the giant food warehouses and the tobacco factory was also blazing.

I do not remember who took over the duties of the civil guard, but Poles wearing some sort of armbands immediately appeared in front of the house entrances, and were telling every passer by to hide in the gateways.

No! I said to myself, I won't sit at home, come what may. I have to see all this! I had on me a 'document' confirming the necessity of my having to move around the town freely, namely I had to carry some wooden crutches for an old man called Papier, a Kraków Bund member, who was in hospital on Kopernik Street at that time and who was unable to go down to the shelter without them. While carrying these crutches, I made my way, along many detours, to the hospital. Along the way I observed the manifestations of this long awaited freedom in its many guises.

Somewhere, I no longer remember the street, three German soldiers were walking. They were wearing helmets and each one of them was carrying an anti-tank weapon. At one point they looked around and saw that the street was totally deserted. They proceeded to stack their 'iron fists' in a little pile, then placed their helmets on top of it and quickly walked off in the opposite direction. A small gravestone marking German glory remained on the roadway. It was a pleasant sight.

In Blich, next to the bridge, stood a wooden hand cart which was loaded up with sacks of sugar. It had been struck by a Soviet bomb. Sugar was pouring out from the torn sacks straight on top of the dead man and was being dyed red with his blood. It was loot from the warehouses which had been destroyed and were burning.

And somewhere else someone had covered three German corpses with a newspaper. A man who had had rather a lot to drink shouted in my direction, 'Come over here, my girl, have a look what dead Krauts look like! I bet you never had the chance to see one during the entire war!' and he moved the newspaper aside. But I had no desire to look at dead Krauts.

As the Germans began to disappear off the streets, the population of Kraków began to emerge, pushing carts and carrying bags and bundles. They were running, walking, carrying heavy boxes, cans and sacks. One in particular has stuck in my memory: he was rolling a large cheese circle along the road as if it were a car wheel. These people were not stealing, but rather were trying to rescue everything possible from the blazing warehouses, everything they had not eaten or seen during the last few years: real coffee, tea, sardines, pickles, but above all, alcoholic drinks, bottles of vodka, cognac, wine, liqueur, everything the heart desires. For two or three days Kraków had no water as the Germans had cut off the mains, but one could have baths in alcohol. Gradually the pavements became covered with rice, biscuits, and bits of glass from broken bottles and window panes.

In Wanda's flat I met 'Baśka' Kowalczyk and together with her and her husband I went out into the street. It was winter and as both of us were rather shabby, what really tempted us were stockings, warm socks and shoes. There was a textile store on the second floor of one of the houses on Mikołajska Street. People were throwing whole bales of material, which were flowing like multicoloured streams, directly into the street. Stockings and warm underwear were also to be found there. But Staszek Kowalczyk had principles, and he would not let us touch anything. In an evangelical tone he was preaching to our frozen souls, 'Girls! Don't do this, this is a historic moment and it must not be stained by earthly considerations. Look and remember . . .', and so on in the same vein.

'Baśka' who always expressed herself simply and bluntly, rebelled: 'If I have to go around with my bottom bare and naked legs, then I have had enough of this historic moment!' But it was to no avail. He would not let us take anything, but on the other hand as we visited all our friends in turn, we were fed all sorts of delicacies. There were piles on every table. People were drinking heavily; they drank your health, to the German

FOR WHOM THE BELLS OF VICTORY TOLLED

defeat, to freedom, to independence which was waiting at the next turn.

One early winter evening, while looking out of the window of some flat, I think it was on Bosacka Street, we saw our first Russians. I had a feeling that I was watching a film, so unreal it seemed. Four Russians were walking down the middle of the road, tall and broad, dressed in white sheepskins and carrying rifles at the ready. They were singing some sad, beautiful song in their strong, low-pitched voices. It was not one of those Russian songs, loud and full of life, which I loved so much. This was not the voice of victors, powerful and joyful. It was a song about a soldier's toil and trouble, drawn out like the snow-covered steppes along which they had walked, fighting and dying. I understood this song even without the words, there was mourning in it, my mourning in these victory days.

By the next day the market was full of soldiers, bonfires were burning and boots and footcloths were drying by them and water was boiling for tea. The Poles were going up to the soldiers to say something nice and to greet them as their saviours and friends. But this did not last long, as only a few days later, a long queue of people with all sorts of complaints had already formed in front of the Main Soviet Command building.

I had quite different complaints during these days of great celebration and even greater muddle. I set off on foot to the cloister to see my Hania. Dead horses were lying on the Bronowice road; the shooting here must have been very intense. These were beautiful horses, not just any old nags. On their way out, the Germans were grabbing choice steeds. Some of them had the best cuts of meat removed. Horse steaks were not to be scorned at a time like this.

As I had no idea where I would be staying myself, I did not want to take my niece to Kraków just yet. All I wanted was to see and to comfort her, to tell her that I existed, that I was alive, and that we would be together before long. But I came upon her in the cellar where, together with other children, she was sorting potatoes. Her hands were frost-bitten, swollen and red. This sight, even though I realised that no injustice was involved, stabbed me to the very depth of my heart.

I made a clumsy attempt to explain to her about my situation, that at this moment I could not . . . . I never finished the sentence. She looked at me with eyes brimming over with tears and moved aside when I tried to embrace her. I felt like a criminal. I packed up her things, her orphan's belongings and I went to thank the mother superior for her care. I thanked her with all my heart, but I did not give away the secret.

We walked back together, not saying one word about the fact that we would both be waiting for someone from now on. We were both afraid of the subject.

I still had to wait many weeks for any news from Hungary, but when it finally arrived, brought by someone who had met Mordecai in Budapest, I knew that I was getting him back. But Hania did not get her father back. I do not even know where he perished, most probably it was in Auschwitz, together with the Hungarian Jews. My parents', Hania's mother's and her elder sister's trail broke off where the railway track to Bełżec breaks off. For a long time afterwards I still nurtured the hope that maybe my brother had managed to survive somewhere in Russia. Refugees began to arrive back from there. But even this bubble of hope burst one day, when a strange woman came up to me and said, 'Your maiden name is Hochberg, isn't it? Well, I can tell you all about how your brother died, I knew him . . .'

APPENDIX

My letter to Dr Berman, undated, probably from the end of 1943:

Dear Mr Berman!

I am sorry for not having replied immediately but I missed the day of Mr Arczyński's departure. I am not going to write anything about the firm's business, as Mr Wójcik is coming. I only wanted to tell you that I received a letter from Bronek's friend, Michał D. who complains of the fact that he cannot get in touch with Antoni, who used to come to visit Bronek on Żelazna Street. As it appears that Bronek parted with his landlady on the best of terms, so it is all right to go there. Anyway, I hope that this affair has been sorted out by now. From our side we are also not very happy, because of financial problems; I am very worried that all our plans and hopes have fallen through. I take this opportunity to remind you about Janina H. from Lwów, she will need some new things for the spring as she has grown quite a lot. Please, try and remember about her. I will get her Memoirs ready for sending before the holidays. Our Ziutka is here in the camp, and one could do so much for our friends and relatives if only one had some money. My best regards to you and to everyone.

Mariańska

[Marek Arczyński – treasurer of the Polish Council Żegota – Warsaw
Władysław Wójcik – secretary of the Polish Council Żegota – Kraków

WITNESSES

Bronek – Bronisław Warman
Michał D – I do not know his surname
'Antoni' – I do not remember whose pseudonym this was
Janina H. – J. Hescheles, refugee from the Janowski Camp]

'An order' from Dr Berman (a copy of a letter from the Dr Berman archive in Lochamej Hagetaot):

We request the following documents:

1) 2 ID cards with addresses in Kraków or other provincial towns, but if only Warsaw ones should be available, then with registration in Kraków or its suburbs, dated the beginning of the current year

2) 2 work certificates, matched up to the ID cards, of the type which would justify freedom of travel on the railways and would also provide exemption from roundups, if possible a cert. (illegible) from the Central Care Council

3) Appropriate work cards

4) A Kraków permit to have freedom of movement in the Pruszkow district, with the place being left blank, if possible, or entered as Laski, Ozarow or Wlochy, for the purposes of searching for one's family. (The bearer of this letter has a pattern for such a permit.)

5) In case we had to use old ID cards, we would need certificates of having gone through selection in a camp and of having been exempted from work. (The bearer of this letter has a pattern of such a certificate.)

Personal details:

1) Michał Biernacki, born 1.3.1902. Krynki Kreis Grodno – clerk

2) Barbara Biernacka, maiden name Borowska, born 20.2.1907. Krynki Kreis Grodno, clerk or child minder

Warsaw K.K.   1) 600080
                               date of issue 2.4.1943
              2) 600081

APPENDIX

address: Krasińskiego 21 flat 22

Attention: please make fingerprints or send us suitable dye

Biernacki Michał – Berman's 'Aryan' name
Borowski Adam – Berman's secret pseudonyms

The next letter about additional documents has been lost, however my reply to it has been preserved in Dr Berman's archive:

Dear Sir!

You cannot imagine how happy I was to get news from you at last. We have been worried about you for a very long time. Because the matter of the documents is so urgent, I have decided not to wait for the Lwów stamps, which will only be available on Wednesday, Thursday, and I am sending you ones from Złoczów, together with a deportation letter. That place was evacuated in April. We do not have any birth certificates from Złoczów, but I do not think that matters, as in recent times people tend to wander from one end of the globe to the other. In the meantime I am including one Lwów blank, with an indifferent signature and I will be sending more as soon as possible.

I received 30 dollars through the via Suchedniów. Thank you very much for remembering me, but at this time I do not need such a sum. I have my salary and I must make it last somehow. As usual, I will turn to you in case of need. I send you and your wife my best regards.

Mariańska

Simultaneously with Dr Berman's requests for documents, I received a letter from his wife Basia:

Dear Mrs Mariańska!

We would like to remind you about the paper and carbon and, in addition, would you please bring us some blank birth certificates from Kraków, registered in different towns, or Warsaw, as may need them for various persons.

19.XI.44　　　　　　　　　Best regards, B. Berman

WITNESSES

One more letter from me to Dr Berman:

Dear Mr Berman!

I was very glad to hear from you. Thank you for remembering me. At first I thought that the matter did not look very promising, but a few days later the situation has become a lot clearer, and it looks like everything will turn out all right.

I think that Kazik will be better able to inform you about his status, one thing however I can tell you that is difficult as serving on committees has always been difficult for me, working in the firm is for me always the first and most important objective. You will get the list of our clients which you asked for, as soon as we manage to bring it up to date. Regards to you and to Mikołaj.

Mariańska

[Kazik – Symcha Rathajzer]

A letter from 10.1.1944 (for the sake of camouflage, the year 1934 is mentioned – a case of very naive mystification, considering the strange content)

My dears!

At last, after a long wait and many reminders, I received your reply confirming the receipt of 30 kg of soap and a promise to send me an answer to my question. I am very happy to get any sign of life from you. So far as your requests are concerned, I would like to assure you that you will receive 100 kg and perhaps even more for our family and our friends, the families Chaimskis and Beczkowskis. It can well be that we will be able to send something or other especially for you, that is for our family and for Tarnowska. Please let us know who has remained with you from our firm and is still working with you from Tarnowska and who has gone and where to do similar work to yours. Let me know if Jurek, Maks's son is somewhere and whether he is working. Perhaps it might be possible to get to see him here, and maybe he could visit our family – I could make this easier for him. If it should not prove possible for you to visit me, I would be glad to

APPENDIX

do something about it. Is Mrs Futrzarska well, is she working , etc. I await your promised letter, as a reply to my first letter and also to this one. Write and tell me what your relationship with our friends and their family is. In conclusion, I enclose the very best regards from myself and my friends for you, the whole family and the Tarnowski relatives.

Yours, Józef

W. 10.1.1934

I find it difficult to decipher the names and pseudonyms in this letter. Perhaps, given the opportunity, one of the Jewish activists from Warsaw, living in this country at the present time, might be able to do it, then I may be able to complete the facts given below. The author was Szymon Gotesman – 'Józef Bogucki'. He is addressing Jewish prisoners in the Płaszowski Camp through the Kraków Council. As far as the 'soap' about which the author of the letter writes is concerned, it is obvious that he is talking about funds – but how many thousands of złotys are involved, I cannot tell. I only know that it concerned additional funds from the National Jewish Committee in Warsaw, which conspicuously used to feed the Kraków Council funds. After the Warsaw uprising in 1944, Szymon Gotesman took on the job of secretary of the Aid Council Żegota, when the group of underground activists found themselves in Milanówek. His next letter, which reached me through the mediation of the contact 'Ewa', originates in this period. This letter was sent to her and was passed on to us for 'deciphering'.

Dear lady!

As I am not certain whether or not Mr Mikołaj passed the case of those of our clients whose names are listed below to you, I am taking the liberty of asking you to take care of these matters in Kraków.

They are: 1-2 Marek Rudnicki and wife, Stradom St. 27/9
3-4 Lola Werchracka and child, into the hands of Mrs Maria Groinska, in the 'Mitropy' office in the Railway Station

In addition, I have asked Marek to look after Mr Bierniarz, whose address I had given to him on a card at that time. Would you kindly remind him of this matter.

P.S. In addition I have personally asked you about Mrs Dąbrowska and her child and Pulaska and her child.

I kiss your hands and I send my best regards to Marek.

Józef Bogucki

The most difficult of all to decipher are Leon Feiner's ('Mikołaj's') letters, which were written in tiny handwriting on small cards. There are two letters directed to the president of the Aid Council Żegota in Kraków, Stanisław Dobrowolski

Letter date 1.XI 1944:

Dear Mr Dobrowolski!

1) Based on the resolution passed by the Regional Council as a centre dated 22/X, would you please send me the exact report of the proceedings on the subject of medicines and other objects from the main Aid Council (conditions, figures, who participated what value, etc. the dates of the dispatches*).

2) Next, I would like you to send me a statement of the copy of the telegram which was sent to L. about the money (and the date it was sent).

3) Finally, I would very much appreciate a detailed report of the work of the Kraków Council during VIII – IX – X (if possible, I would like to request copies of the records and a detailed report of the liquidation of the Płaszow Camp).

I thank you in advance for your cooperation in all these matters, and I send you my very best regards.

1.XI 44

On the side there is a note: * 'because Lon. is asking'.

On the reverse side of the same card:

Would you please tell comrade Mariańska that I received her and Kazik's letter and that I am in contact with Bogucki from National Żegota, who has joined the

APPENDIX

Warsaw Council in place of Adam, and that I do everything to make his work easier in every respect (also financially) – I expect that one need have no anxieties about the finances. If we get those from Del. and divide our own fairly, there will be enough for the others. We will take care of these matters when someone comes to see me. Please send me a report of all the activities. Best regards

Mikołaj

Medicines and other objects from the Central Care Council has to do with items sent from abroad care of Dr Weichert.

The telegram referred to was handed over to me by Stefan Grajek and Józef Sak and it said:

Ing. Reiss – Dr Schwarzbard

New clusters of Jews who after leaving Warsaw continue to find themselves in appalling conditions remain. We have no money. Send considerable funds immediately. I still do not know the fate of those dearest to me.

Grajek

There was still another telegram, with a similar content, signed Stefan, Józef, but I no longer have that one. I gave it to Professor Seweryn, who was supposed to send it to London via a secret broadcasting station with the help of the Land Army, I think.

Letter dated 17 XI 1944

Dear Stanisław!

Please reply to my letter written over a month ago. In addition, please come to pick up the money for the Council. Furthermore, I would like Mariańska to reply to the letter which I addressed to her. Let us know if any significant amount of money has come for us. I await a prompt reply via the same way [illegible] the previous letter and also this one. Best regards

Mikołaj

17 XI 44

I am citing the letters below, not always in their actual order, as not all of them are dated. They were addressed to Wójcik and to me.

> Dear Sir,
>
> As a member of the Central Aid Council, I wish to express my heart-felt thanks for the efforts and the help you have extended on our behalf. I hope to be able to express these thanks in the next few days in person. The money which we have received thanks to you, is being used to help a dozen or so refugees who happen to be in the same place where we are starving. But there also is a large number of refugees around Częstochowa and in the entire Kielce district. Some sort of help for them is indispensable, if they are not to face total extinction. I am taking the liberty of turning to you with the request to make available a considerable sum of money to the Central Aid Council, to make it possible for us to carry out this action.
>
> As Mrs Mariańska is planning to come and see us in a few days time, I will come to Kraków after having seen Mrs Mariańska.
>
> In the hope that you will be continuing with your initial efforts, I remain yours
>
> Stefan
>
> P.S. We discussed certain matters with Mrs Mariańska, which she will recount to you in person.

The constant reference to the Central Aid Council was a camouflage, as in reality a secret Jewish organisation was involved. In this instance the camouflage was extremely naive. If, God forbid, the Germans would have stopped me with one of these letters on me, but without any official document stating that I was a Central Aid Council worker, and in addition, with such an amount of money, as well as ID cards, seals, etc, my fate would have been sealed.

'Kazik' or Symcha Rathajzer had added one page to the above cited letter as follows.

> Dear Sir!
>
> I am most grateful to you for the help extended to us. I

APPENDIX

hope that you will continue to make attempts to obtain a more substantial sum of money for our branch of the Central Aid Council.

We desperately need money for the carrying out [illegible] aid action for our close family. I was genuinely delighted that Mrs Mariańska came to see us, and in future I would like to ask you to arrange any contacts between us through Mrs Mariańska. However, I hope to see you soon. Best regards

Kazik

Next, there are three letters from Grajek addressed to me.

Dear Mrs Mariańska!

We very much regret the fact that for a long time now we have had no opportunity of direct contact with you. We also think that it would be very useful if you would come to see us, as this would make it possible for us to discuss many matters which cannot be solved in writing.

Borowski sends his heartfelt greetings. We will, most probably, receive a detailed letter from him to you in the near future, which we will send on to you without delay.

Borowski begged that the matters relating to documents should be taken care of immediately, if at all possible, as they are urgently needed. As for ourselves, we would like to ask you for several birth certificates from Warsaw and from the provinces in blank form. In K.N.'s name we are sending 30 dollars for your use, which were received from Borowski for this purpose, before we and he managed to make contact with Milanówek.

We send our best regards in expectation
Józef and Stefan

Dear colleague!

It is more than a week now since we have had any news from you. I made plans to come and see you, but because of the dangers involved with the journey (especially during the last few days) I had to postpone my departure.

For this reason Marysia is now coming to see you and I hope that you will come to see us soon.

I would very much like to know how all the matters which we had discussed are progressing and I would like to ask you to write me all about it. Has anyone come from Warsaw as yet?

I should like to ask you to try and get some sort of reasonable certificate for me, which would make my work easier. Is there perhaps a letter from Michał for me? I await your reply and your visit. Best regards

Stefan

[Marysia – Maria Sawicka]

We expected you last week, but you did not come. Please be kind enough to tell Marysia when you are intending to come.

Now some more requests: we include several photos and personal details:

The documents for the first four persons (Marysia, Hajdas – a woman from Moniecpole, Dutkiewicz and me) are very urgent and we beg you to try and get them done on Sunday, or Monday at the latest, as everyone of these persons has to travel to look after our matters. Hajdas and Dutkiewicz have no documents of any kind.

We would also like you to inform us whether or not our telegrams were sent off and if any answer to them has arrived. Awaiting your reply, we send our best regards

Józef Stefan

P.S. Marysia and I are going to Milanówek for the holidays. If you find you wish to send anything for anyone, please tell Marysia about it.

Stefan

FINANCIAL MATTERS

I am not able to give precise information about the Kraków Council's financial matters. These were discussed in special meetings in which I did not take part. The details connected

APPENDIX

with the question how the aid to Jews was financed, can be found in various published works, among them Władysław Bartoszewski's book, *This One is From My Country* (Kraków 1966, 1st edition) and Mark Arczyński's and Wiesław Balcerak's *The Cryptonym 'Żegota'*. References can also be found in *The History of Aid to Jews in Poland 1939-1945* (Warsaw 1979, 1st edition), Tatiana Berenstein's and Adam Rutkowski's *Aid for Jews in Poland, 1939-1945* (Warsaw 1963); and the recently published and carefully prepared book by Teresa Prekerowa, *The Secret Council for Jewish Aid in Warsaw 1942-1945* (Warsaw 1982).

It seems, from my own experiences, as well as from many of the letters cited here, that 'calls' for greater allowances for the Kraków Council never stopped. The money from London was being transferred by drops which the Home Army retrieved in places previously indicated by secret radio messages. Instructions on how the dollars were to be distributed were given by the same radio channels. So far as I know, no one has so far determined how much of this money got lost on the way.

According to the receipts which survived in our archive and are partially published here, signed by the charges, during the period 1943-4, each person was paid 1,000 złotys a month, without taking into account any one-off amounts, like those for 'winter aid', i.e. coal and clothing, or special expenses, such as in the case of the 'refugee from Auschwitz', when considerably larger quotas were involved. During the first year of our work in the Kraków Council for Jewish Aid, the allowances were considerably lower, more like 300-500 złotys a month.

The Kraków Council funds were also supported to a large extent by the secret Jewish National Committee and by the Bund. I have no information on how these funds managed to reach the organisations in question. I do not know whether they went via the delegates of the Polish Government in London or via some other means. The copy of the telegram to London, signed by Stefan Grajek and addressed to Dr Schwarzbard and Ing. Reiss, who were Jewish activists abroad, sheds some light on this subject.

The fact that I was able to hand Grajek 50,000 złotys from the Kraków Council's funds in October 1944, as well as other documents (Lieberman's statement about 25,000 złotys for

177

'winter aid' for the ten Jews in the bunker) proves that at that time we possessed considerable amounts of money. Some of this money also came from the sale of products which had been stored in the 'Jus' warehouses, when Dr Weichert was forced to give up his activities.

As I have already mentioned above, I kept many receipts for sums paid out to charges, and I enclose copies of a small part of these receipts here. For the sake of secrecy, for the most part, the sums shown on them have the final two zeros missing and are dated ten years earlier. According to the description which was based on these same receipts, 226 people were receiving aid. But, once again, I must underline the fact that I managed to preserve only a small part of the receipts. According to reports contained in various publications (including those listed above), there were more than one thousand persons which the Council was helping during this period in the city, its surroundings and in the camps.

INDEX

Aid to Jews in Poland 177
Albertine Convent 54-6
Alcohol Monopoly 88
Aleksandrowicz, Jerzyk 110-11
Aleksandrowicz, Julian 110-11, 120
Aleksandrowicz, Marylka 110-11
Anashim ve Efer (Gutman) 136
Andrzejek 24, 25
Ania O. 114-15, 138-40, 143
anti-semitism xi, 10-11, 57-8, 103
Arbeitsamt 23
Arczyński, Marek 80, 134, 152, 167, 177
armbands xiii, 4, 12, 15, 50
Aryan documents xiv, 11, 29, 35-6, 39 *see also* identity documents
Aryan looks xi, xiv, 11-12, 19
'Aryan side' xi, xv-xvi, xvii
Auschwitz 91, 114, 127, 177; Szymon Zajdów story 136-41

Balcerak, Wiesław 177
Bartoszewski, Władysław 78, 161, 177
Bauminger, Arie 147
Beczkowski family 170
Beer, Moishe 2
Bekanntmachungen (edicts) xii-xiii
Belgium (occupation) 16
Bełżec 35, 41, 48-52, 70, 161, 166

Berenstein, Tatiana 177
Berman, Basia 169
Berman, Dr 88, 152, 167-70
Bernstein (photographer) 13
Biała Góra 12
Bielsko 34-5, 161
Biernacka, Barbara 168
Biernacki, Michał 168-9
Bierniarz, Mr 172
Bilewicz, Tadeusz 76
Bircza, 12 13
Birken, Józek (Józef Kowalik) 58-9
Birnbaum, Dawid 5, 53
Birnbaum, Litka 35, 51-2, 98
Birnbaum family 35, 47-8, 98, 99
birth certificates 159-60
'Bizanc' cafe 65
black market 118
blackmailers xv, xvii, 19
Blich 163
'Blitzkrieg' 64
blue documents 4
Bobrowski, Maria 102
Bobrowski, Mieczysław (Mietek) 102, 104, 105, 108
Bocheńska Street 27
Bochnia 22, 52
Bojko (Ukrainian policeman) 26-7, 98
Borek Fałęcki 42
Boruchowicz, Max 72-9, 125, 132, 154

179

INDEX

Bosacka Street 165
bread (trade in) 15, 27-8, 85
Bronek 167
Bronia 14, 148
Bronowice 54, 86, 120, 127, 165
Bund 87, 103, 115, 156, 158, 163, 177

Camus, Albert *The Plague*, 124-5
Carmelite Convent 1
case-histories (importance) xii
Catholic religion xv, 10, 23-4, 61-4, 92-3
Central Aid Council 174-5
Central Care Council 91, 168, 173
Chaimski family 170
children: borrowed (during searches) 148-9; orphaned after Bełżec) 52-6; in Poronin orphanage 133-4
Christmas customs 62
churches (as rendezvous) 63
Churchill, Winston S. 16-17
cigarettes (trade in) 15, 27
City Council (Kraków) 140
City Council (Tarnów) 4
Clothiers' Hall 5
coal chests (use of) 86-8
collaborators 150
Committee of Auditors 84
concentration camps xiii
concierges 28, 99, 117
confession (by Catholics) 63, 159
Council for Jewish Aid xi, xvii, 29, 59, 125; financial matters 176-8; Janka Hescheles' story 132, 133; in Kraków 23-4, 27, 53, 74-5, 171-2; in Kraków (first steps) 80-93; in Kraków (new contacts/methods) 103, 108, 114; Ogrodowa Street cellar 142, 144; Szymon Zajdów story 136; in Warsaw 80-4, 152, 154, 167
County Council 3
crematoria xiii
'Cryptonym "Żegota"', The' 134, 177

cyanide capsules 18, 77
Cyrankiewicz, Józef, 65, 78, 91; arrest 11, 15, 18, 22, 89; Auschwitz 127, 136; early activities 4-6, 9, 11, 14-15, 18-19, 22
Czarna 69
Czarnowiejska Street 117
Częstochowa 174

D., Michał 167, 168
D., Mrs (landlady) 7, 9-11, 18, 131, 133
Dąbrowska, Mrs 172
death camps xv, 29
death rate xiii
Dębica 1, 51, 52, 148
Dębniki 27, 54, 79, 100, 114, 138-9
Decree (of 10 December 1942) xvi-xvii
Dekel, Efraim 121
Democratic Party 84
Denmark (surrender) 16
Dietla Street 54, 130, 138, 146
Długa Street 43, 109
Dobrowolska, Anna (Michalska) 82-4, 133, 144
Dobrowolski, Stanisław (Staniewski) 81-2, 86, 88, 92, 102, 113, 172-3
document factory 130-1, 153
dogs (use of) 76
Drobner, Bolesław 88
Drobnerowa 88

East (movements) 2, 3, 6, 31
Easter customs 62, 63
economy, destruction of xiii
'Edyś' 27, 90
Eizman, Jehuda (Landenheim) 74n
Emil (hospital worker) 21-2
English radio 7, 16-17, 145
Estreicher, Karol 91
'Ewa' (Miriam as) 9, 171
exemption certificates 89-90
extermination camps xiii
extortionists 19

180

INDEX

eye-witness accounts (role) xii
Fannenstein (factory director) 36–8
Feiner, Leon (Mikołaj) 152, 172
Feliks 104
Feuer, Nisan (Jan Kasprzycki) 42–4
financial matters and funding 15, 23–5, 82, 85–6, 114, 118–20, 133, 142–5, 158, 170, 171, 176–8
fingerprints 60
Fischer, Danuta 8
Fischer, Mrs 8
Fischgrund, Maks (Misiołek) 103–5, 107, 108–9, 156
Fischgrund, Salo 103, 146–7, 152
Florek 114, 115
food coupons 15, 27, 28 85
food smuggling 149–50
'forbidden' streets/places 5
Frank, Governor 102
Friedman, Stefa 117, 119
Frimerman, Milek 98
From Beneath the Gallows and into Battle (Borwicz) 77, 78
Fryda 103
fugitives from Janowski 72–9
fur coats 64–5, 69, 70, 71
Futrzarska, Mrs 171

G., Mr (music teacher) 35
Garbarska Street 88, 117
Garbien, Dr 158–9
Gelblum, Irena 153, 154–6
gendarmes, German 67–8, 106, 116
General Government xvii, 4, 127
General Zionist Party 152
German Army 64, 127; entry into Kraków xii, 16; retreat from Kraków 162–6
German language 68
German Philharmonic Orchestra 101–2
Gestapo 18, 26, 69, 76, 102, 119
ghetto-dwellers xv, xvi–xvii

ghettos xiii; Aryan side xv–xvi, xvii
Ginwill-Piotrowski, Kazimierz (Piotrus) 7, 8
Goniec Krakówski 16
Górska, Maria (Miriam as) 6
Gotesman, Szymon (Józef Bogucki) 152, 170–1, 172, 175
Governor General xvi–xvii
Grajek, Stefan 84, 116, 152–4, 173, 174–5, 177
green documents 4
Gregorczyk family 12
Groinska, Maria 171
Gross, Zygmunt 65–6
Grubner, Julian 35, 37–8, 40–1, 47, 73, 76, 97
Grubner, Katia 97–102
Grynberg, Dr 21
Grzegórzki 114
Gutman, Israel 136
Guzik 13

H., Janiana 167
H. J. 161
'Hagada' 115
Hanukah holiday 62
Hanusia 114, 115, 143
Hasidei Umot Haolam 121
Heller, Dr 134
Hering (factory manager) 36
Hescheles, Henryk 79, 133
Hescheles, Janina 167–8
Hescheles, Janka 79, 125; wanderings of 131–5
History of Aid to Jews in Poland, The 177
Hitler, A. 57, 64, 124
Hochberg, Hela 86
Hochberg, Mituśka 53, 86–7
Hochberg, Zygmunt 86
Hochberg family 2–3, 6, 21, 51
Hofman, Jan (Mr Nowak) 24–5
Holland (occupation) 16
Holocaust xi, 5, 56, 96, 161
Holub (factory driver) 36, 44, 76
Holzer, Cesia 4, 32; brother of 32, 33
Home Army 115, 142, 177

181

INDEX

Hrabykowa, Maria (Dzurzyńska) 90-1, 117
humanism 103
Hungarian Jews 141
Hungary 125-6, 166

identity documents 12, 23; document factory 130-1, 153; forged xvii, 4, 27, 29-30, 107
Kennkarten 22, 25-7, 29-30, 52, 59-62, 64-7, 71, 153; legitimation office 85, 88, 129, 148, 156; from Warsaw 148, 159-60
information bulletins 16
informers xv, 19, 34, 150
interrogations 18
Israel, Maier 13
Israel (in Wieliczka) 103

Jabłonowski, Prince 161
Jackowski 105-8, 117
Jagiellońska Street 74n, 81, 82, 92
Janiczek 27, 28-9
Janka (from Bronowice) 23, 54, 86
Janowska Street, 78, 95
Janowska, Wanda 54, 79, 85, 87-8, 129-35, 164
Janowski, Władysław 87
Janowski Camp 36, 41, 94-5, 97, 124-5, 131, 168; fugitives from 72-9
Jedynak, Józef (Grandfather) 102-5, 134
Jedynak, Józia 103
Jedynak, Wanda 103
Jewish Council of Elders 15
Jewish Historical Commission 131, 147
Jewish Hospital 64-5
Jewish National Committee 43-4, 56, 109, 143, 146-7, 152, 171, 177
Jewish Relief Council see Council for Jewish Aid
Jewish Workers' Party (Bund) 87, 103, 115, 156, 158, 163, 177

Jodłowski, Marian 26
Joffe, Dr 115-16
Józefa, Sister 23-4
Judenrat 15, 72
Judenrein status 20, 26, 36, 48
Jurek 170
'Just Among the Nations' xvi, 121

Karmelicka Street 8, 14, 60
Katowice 34
Kennkarten, see identity documents
Kielce ghetto 65, 66
Kielce region 116, 153-5, 157, 174
Klier Fraulein (factory manager) 36, 44
Kłopotowski, Zygmunt 72, 78, 85; activist/friend of the Jews 11, 31-2, 39-40; 41-2; arrest 11, 125; clients 58, 59-63, 65; instructions from 47, 52, 54; leadership 15-16, 18-19, 22, 28-30
Kobyliński family 131, 132
Köller (factory director) 36, 76, 94
Komorowski, Bor 16
Komsomol 32
Konopnicka, Maria 93
'Konrad' 142
Kopernik Street 163
Korn, Mundek 108-9
Kowalczyk, Hanka (Baśka) 137-8, 164
Kowalczyk, Staszek 164
Kowalski, Adam (Konski) 115, 142-7
Krajewska, Hanka 22, 40, 46
Krajewski, Bolek 40
Krajewski family 21, 87
Kraków; Council for Jewish Aid in, see Council for Jewish Aid; early months 5-12; German entry xii; German retreat 162-6; in 1940, 14-18; liquidation and after 46-8, 52-6, 124; new contacts/methods 97-122; spring 1941 18-21;

182

INDEX

-Tarnów-Lwów journeys 31-45
winter 1941-2 21-5
Krakowska Street 98-9, 130
Krakówski Park 113
Kraus (Hirsch) brothers 12
Kreishauptmannschaft 105
Kruczkowska, Adam 54, 130
Kruczkowska, Jadwiga 54, 104-5, 111, 126, 130
Kruczkowska, Leon 54, 130
Kruczkowska, Wanda 111
Krysia 108-10
Krysztal café 9, 65
Kubiczek, Edyś 27, 90
Kuśnierz, Helena 160
KZ xiii

Labour Office 90-1
Land Army 173
Langrod, Bronisława (Bronia) 14, 148
Langsam 12
Lasocka, Teresa (Tell) 91-3, 136, 158
Laufer, Mrs (Krysia's mother) 108-10
Lednica Górna 103
legitimation office 85, 88, 129, 148, 156
Leinkram, Irena 158-9
Leinkram, Leopold 108, 156-9
Leki Dolne 3
Leser, Jona 120
Lesko 12
Lewin, Rabbi 133
Liban Camp 92-3
Lieberman family 115, 142-6, 162
Liegenschaften 107
Lipiny 1
Lisiewicz, Paweł 78
Little Market 7, 9-10, 18, 131, 133
Lochamej Hagetaot 168
London radio 7, 16-17, 145
Lonia, Fraulein (governess) 2-21
looting xiii, 163
Lorek family 39-41

Lublin 147
Lwów 12-14, 94-6, 125;
Kraków-Tarnów journey 31-45

Madritsch Company 53, 86
Maginot line 16
Main Market 53
Main Square 5
Makarsi 12
Maks 170
Mały Rynek 7, 9-10, 18, 131, 133
man-hunts xiii
Mandel family 39-41
Margulies, Henryk 106
Marynia (Szlapak housekeeper) 89
Mass (celebration of) xv, 92-3
Matus, Jerzy 85
Matusowa, Elza 113-14, 115
Matyj, Jadzia 3
Medical Survey 78
Mehl, Niuśka 86
Meisel, Józef 136
Michałowice, 17, 25
Mieczysław Piotrowski, Józef 3, 4
Migdal family 41
Mikołajska Street 164
Milanówek 87, 171, 175
'Mitropy' office 171
Mogilany 142-7
Molnicka, Helena 88-9
Moment 79
money: surrender of xiii; *see also* financial matters and funding
Mościce 58
Moskalska, Alicja 116-17
Motyka, Lucjan 78
Mroczkowski (photographer) 13
Mulner, Jakub 105

National Jewish Committee 43-4, 56, 109, 143, 146-7, 152, 171, 177
Nelken, Wanda 4
New Journal 81
Niedziela family 70

183

INDEX

Niesel und Kämmer 35–41, 44–5, 73, 74n, 76
Niewiara (tailor) 117–22 *passim*
Norway 16
NSDAP 20
Nussbaum, Genia (Bornstein) 117–22

O., Ania 114–15, 138–40, 143
Ogrodowa Street 142–7
Ojców 114
'Organisation Todt' 155
Ortzman, Monek 41–2
Osiedle Oficerskie 23, 156, 158
Osiek, Dr Bernard 52

Palonka, Leon 103
Panna Maria Street 47, 49
Papier (of Kraków Bund) 163
Paris (fall) 16
Peasant Party 84, 85
Peleg, Juda 31
Peleg, Mordecai ix–x, xiv–xvii, 3; Aryan identity 4–6, 35–6; clients, 57–9; on deportations to Bełzec 46–8; early activities, 12–14; on Janówski fugitives 72–9; Kłopotowski's role 29–30; Kraków–Lwów journeys 31–45; Kraków (new contacts/methods) 97–101; personal experiences 123–6; registered addresses 25–9
Peleg-Mariańska, Miriam ix, xiv–xv, xvii; Aryan identity, 1–3; cellar story 142–7; clients 59–71; on deportations to Bełzec 48–52; early activities 5–12; family possessions 69, 70–1; on German retreat, 162–6; Janka's story 129–35; Kraków (1940) 14–18; Kraków (spring 1941) 18–21; Kraków (winter 1941–2) 21–5; new contacts/methods 101–22; on orphaned children 52–6; personal experiences 123–6; Warsaw (contacts with) 148–61; written memories 94–6;

Zajdów's story 136–41
People and Ashes (Gutman) 136
People of the Book xii
personal freedom (restriction) xiii, 5, 16
Philharmonia 101–2
'philo-semitism' 103
Pilzno, 1–3, 15, 47–8, 50–2, 69, 159, 161
'Piotrus' 7, 8
placówka legalizacyjna 11
Planty Park 5
Płaszów Camp xiii, 83, 86, 92, 109, 114, 116, 152, 171, 172
Pod Baranami building 140
Podgórze 53, 88, 98, 130, 131
Podhale 28
Polish anti-semitism xi, 10–11, 57–8
Polish Army, 2, 58
Polish–Jewish relations xi, xv–xvii, 19–20
Polish Main Protection Council 133
Polish police 149–50
Polish Socialist Party 11, 15, 26, 64, 77–8, 81–2, 84–6, 117, 140
Polish speech/behaviour xv
Polish Workers' Party 140
Poronin orphanage 133–5
posters 49–50, 151
prayers/ritual (learning) xv, 61–4
Prekerowa, Teresa, 177
propaganda 151
Pruszkow district 168
Przemyśl 12, 34
Przetaczek family 103
Przybory Estate 161
Przybyszów 1, 22, 47
Pulaska 172
Pustkowie 51

radio communiqués 7–9, 16–17, 145
railway stations 34, 47, 69
Rathjazer, Symcha (Kazik) 153–6, 158, 170, 172, 174–5
rations (and food coupons) 15, 27, 28, 38, 85

INDEX

recruitment 82
Red Army 90, 91, 141; German retreat 162-6
Ref, Count 161
refugees (after Warsaw uprising) 153
Reich, Hania 52-6, 69, 130, 165-6
Reiss, Ing. 173, 177
Rokito 6
Rosieński, Janek (Antoni) 8-9, 167-8
Równe Wołyńskie 6
Rozenberg-Rosieńska, Mrs 8
RPZ, see Council for Jewish Aid
Rudnicki, Marek (and his wife) 171-2
Rutkowski, Adam 177
Ryczów 127
Rymer family 51
Rysiewicz, Adam (Teodor) 26, 43, 68-9, 113, 125-6, 129, 151-2; Auschwitz refugees 136, 140 Council activities 80, 85, 88-9, 93; Janówski fugitives 72-3, 78; murder of 11, 127
Rysiewicz, Jadwiga (Zocha) 87
Rysińska, Ziutka 52-4, 69, 74n, 76, 78-9, 86, 125, 132, 148, 159, 167
Rząska 54
Rzeszów 90, 128

Sącz 113
Sak, Józef 84, 152-3, 173
salt mines 103
Sambor 31
Saski Gardens 151
Sasula, Bronek 26
Saved from Extinction (Dekel) 121
Sawicka, Marysia 116, 153, 154
Schaechter, Sianka 31
Schlosser (clairvoyant) 33
Schneider, Rela 88
Schönberg, Natek 72
Schornstein, Berta 5, 17
Schornstein family 17, 117
Schwarzbard, Dr 64, 177

Schwarzbard family 65
Schweiger, Inka 87
Sebastian Street 102
Secret Council for Jewish Aid in Warsaw, The (Prekerowa) 177
security measures (underground) 17-18
Seiden, Mrs Tonia 57-8
Seifert, Henia 161
Seifert, Zygmunt 161
semitic looks 26, 137
Seweryn, Professor Tadeusz (Socha) 78, 84, 173
shames (priest) 2
shops (marking of) xiii
Siemiradzka Street 113, 158
Skała 114
Skarżysko-Kamienna 100
Skarżysko Camp 105
Skawińska Street 21-2, 40, 87
Skazowa, Zofia 53-4
skis (confiscation) 64
Skosowski, Lolek 152
Śląsk 140
slave labour xiii, 103
Słomniki 162
Słoneczna Street 77
Słowacki Theatre 91
smuggling 149-50
Soviet-German border 12-13, 31-2
Soviet Army 32, 90, 91, 141; German retreat 162-6
Sprecher family 12, 14
SS units 2, 49, 59, 76, 95
Stalingrad 124
Star of David xiii, 4, 12
Starowiślna Street 26-7, 54, 86, 97, 99, 146
Staszek (factory worker) 38-9
Staszek (taxi driver) 5
Stefan, Józef 175-6
Steinbach, Mieczysław (Mietek) 4-7
Sternfeld family 26
stool-pigeons 150, 152
Stradom Street 25-6, 171
Strzałecka, Jadwiga 133-5
Strzałecki, Janusz 84

INDEX

Suchedniów 116, 154, 169
Suchniów 153
swastika 75
Szeptycki, Metropolita 133
Szlapak, Dr Helena 80, 88–90, 91, 93, 117, 158
szmalcownicy 19

T. family 58–9
Targówek 159
Tarnów xiv, 1, 4–5; deportation to Bełzec 47–50; Kraków–Lwów journey 31–45
Tarnowska 170, 171
telegram transmitter 84
This One is From My Country (Bartoszewski) 78, 161, 177
Through the Eyes of a Twelve-year-old Girl (Hescheles) 131–2
Tisch (German) 86
Toras (protection of) 2
travel restrictions xiii, 5, 16
Treibicz, Bela 159–60, 161
Treibicz, Dziunek 159, 160–1
trench digging 89–90
Tuchów 42

Ukrainians 32, 34, 38
underground: materials/paper 7–8, 14, 16, 17; Polish Socialist Party 11, 15, 26, 64, 77–8, 81–2, 84–6, 117, 140; security measures 17–18; Żegota, *see* Council for Jewish Aid
Union for the Armed Struggle 29
Ursuline Convent 23–4

valuables (confiscation) xiii
Vistula River 46, 60
Volkdeutsch 8, 15
'voluntary resettlement' orders 16, 17; Warsaw 46–8

Wałowa Street 12, 49
Warman, Bronisław (Bronek) 167–8
Warsaw 66; contacts with 148–61; Council 80–4, 152, 154, 167; uprising 116, 118, 143, 153, 171
Wcisło, Jan 86–7
Wcisło family, 54, 87, 99
Weichert, Dr 173, 178
Weksler, Hanka 117
Werchracka, Lola (and her child) 171
Wieliczka 17, 53, 102–3, 107–13, 130, 137, 138
Wielopole Street 83, 163
Wilhaus (camp commander) 74n
'winter aid' 177, 178
Wisła River 138, 139
Wodzisław 157
Wójcik, Władek 102, 105, 167; Auschwitz refugees, 136–7; Council activities 59, 84–8, 152–4, 158; Janka's story 129, 131; Janowski fugitives 75, 77–8
Wojnarek, Kazimierz (Szymon Zajdów) 91, 114, 136–41
Wojnarowicz, Wacław (Leopold Leinkram) 108, 156–9
Wolnica Square 99
Wolnica 162
Wolność 7, 14
Wołyń 6
work camps xiii
work certificates 91
Woźnik, Władysław 91
Wrzesińska Street 87, 88, 130
Wygoda 70
Wyspianski, Professor 140

Yad Vashem 53–4, 116–17, 136, 156
Yiddish language 41, 68

Zając, Helena 61–3
Zajdów, Szymon 91, 114, 136–41
Załnż 12, 14
Zamarstynowska Street 41
Zblitowska Góra 48
Żegota, *see* Council for Jewish Aid

186

INDEX

Żelazna Street 167
Zielna Street 27, 100, 112
Zielona Street 35, 38
Zionists 80-1, 152
Złoczów 169
Zofia, Madame 8

Żoliborz 66
Żołkiew 32
Żurawia Street 152
Zweig, Arnold 131
Związek Walki Zbrojnej 29
Zyklon B. xiii